TUNING THE CLASSIC MINI

TUNING THE CLASSIC MINI

CLIVE TRICKEY

MRP

Motor Racing Publications Limited
Unit 6, The Pilton Estate, 46 Pitlake, Croydon, CR0 3RA, England

Tuning the Mini first published 1966
More Mini Tuning first published 1968
This combined and revised edition published 1991

British Library Cataloguing in Publication Data
   Trickey, Clive
   Tuning the classic mini.
   I. Title
   629.2222

   ISBN 0947981616

Typeset by Ryburn Typesetting Ltd; origination by Ryburn Reprographics, Halifax, West Yorkshire

Printed in Great Britain by
The Amadeus Press Limited, Huddersfield, West Yorkshire

Contents

Foreword

An introduction to this book from the publisher

The Mini is one of a small number of cars, among the countless models which make up the hundred-year history of motoring, which have truly acquired cult status. It is not merely a matter of fashion, though a spell in the fashionable spotlight as an accoutrement of the rich and famous was one early indicator of the Mini's success. More than that, it is the quality which inspires a dedicated band of followers to devote their loyalty, enthusiasm, time and money to the car, and to go on doing so without regard to developments in engineering and changes in style taking place elsewhere. It has led them to use the Mini not only on the road but also in just about every conceivable form of motorsport, to modify and convert it in many different ways, sometimes almost beyond recognition, and to take it as a basis for a whole variety of kit cars and specials.

Partly, of course, it is because the car is cheap, simple and mostly easy to work on. Partly, it can be explained by the fact that the Mini was in many ways a revolutionary design, proving to be the forerunner of a type which has become one of the mainstays of much of the world's motor industry, the small, transverse-engined, front-wheel-drive, two-box saloon. But it goes beyond such rather academic definitions into the much harder-to-define areas of character and charm. Certainly, it would have been hard to foresee such a very long career ahead of the model when it made its debut before a startled public in 1959.

After the passage of so many years, it is perhaps necessary to remind older readers, and to explain to some of the younger ones, that when the Mini first appeared it had either Morris Mini Minor or Austin Seven badges. The 'Seven' name never caught on, perhaps because the pre-war Austin Seven was itself a car of such distinctive character that it has a fanatical following to this day. 'Minor' was closely associated with another Morris model too, and consequently, although separate Austin and Morris identities persisted for some time, the new baby very quickly became just 'Mini' to everybody. It was the product of an outfit called the British Motor Corporation, universally known as BMC. Sundry mergers and other corporate machinations subsequently transformed the company into the British Leyland Motor Corporation (BLMC), later known simply as British Leyland (BL). The marketing men then made Mini a marque in its own right, distinct from Austin and Morris, and the latter name died with the end of Ital (née Marina) production. When portions of the state-owned BL agglomeration were hived off into separate ownership, the Mini found itself the property of the Austin Rover Group (ARG), which was in turn acquired by British Aerospace in 1988. The Austin name too faded from the scene, but the Mini soldiered on through a long twilight and out into a new glow of popularity. The recent launch of a reborn Mini-Cooper emphasizes how the little car has endured long enough to profit by the nostalgia for its own past, a feat achieved by very few other mass-produced models.

So while some people are still enjoying buying and driving bright new Minis, others are caring for older ones and reliving, in events like historic rallies, the great era when the smaller-capacity classes in saloon-car racing were full of tyre-smoking Minis and the Cooper S was a force to be reckoned with in international rallying. It is those earlier days we are concerned with in these pages.

The late Clive Trickey was a doyen of the first wave of Mini fanatics, an amateur tuner and racing driver for whom the word 'enthusiastic' is really inadequate. *Cars and Car Conversions* was the magazine which any club motorsport participant with an interest in the technical and practical aspects of the sport had to read (as it still is today): when Trickey wrote to correct something the magazine published about the Mini, then-editor Martyn Watkins said, in effect, 'If you think you can do better, you write the Mini articles for us!' Trickey did, and it was the beginning of a long-running series followed particularly keenly by those who, like Trickey himself, were preparing their own Minis for competition on a limited budget. The articles were eventually collected together in two books, *Tuning the Mini* and *More Mini Tuning*.

In deciding to publish this combined edition, we have been influenced both by the demand for the original titles, continuing long after they were both out of print, and by the renewed interest in the heyday of the competition Mini. What follows is both a source of practical information for anyone tuning an earlier Mini and an insight into the world of Minis in club motorsport in the 1960s. While we have taken the opportunity to re-arrange the material in a more logical sequence and to eliminate one or two glaring contradictions, we have largely resisted the temptation to update or apply the wisdom of hindsight, anxious to preserve the essential character of the original.

Clive Trickey's enthusiasm for the Mini was boundless: 'truly one of the most versatile, tunable and exciting mass-produced cheap motor cars ever made,' he called it, 'a credit to its designer, the technical brilliance of the British Motor Corporation and British industry as a whole.' But his love did not blind him to the car's faults, as the repeated references to weaknesses and failures makes clear. His was an essentially practical standpoint, as he was at pains to explain: 'It may be thought by some people that I have been unduly critical of the various types of Mini, and that the weakness and faults mentioned are trifling and uncommon. I have done this deliberately, not to discourage but to warn that enthusiasm should always be tempered by moderation, and unless one considers any possible pitfalls carefully before carrying out modifications, one can be landed with a most unpleasant surprise such as a badly bent or blown-up motor car.

'I would say that my knowledge of these weaknesses does not discourage my enthusiasm, for I think the Mini is a fabulous motor car, having in fact far fewer faults than most of its contemporaries.'

He was, clearly, not shy of venturing an opinion, and hand-in-hand with his fervent advocacy of the Mini went a dedication to the idea that the keen amateur tuner, able to expend almost unlimited time and energy on a project, could equal or better many of the achievements of the professional tuning shops at far less cost. In his introduction to the third edition of *Tuning the Mini*, he wrote: 'What I have tried to do is show that the theories and principles of modifying any motor car are not some kind of mumbo-jumbo for long-haired boffins only. Any fairly competent do-it-yourself enthusiast can, with a little forethought and careful application to the job in hand, greatly increase the performance of his vehicle . . .' That capacity for taking pains, a delight in finding low-cost, if sometimes laborious, alternatives to the money-no-object approach, is evident throughout and much of the advice is as valid today as it was when first written. Above all, Trickey was no mere theorist: what he wrote about, he had tried and tested in competition himself, and his 850 racer, KTR 223E, was a front-runner in the Mini-7 formula.

For anyone interested in tuning a classic Mini in the 1990s, all kinds of useful lessons can be learned from Trickey's experience. Some fundamental points must always be borne in mind. It is important to read the whole book before trying to apply any parts of it in isolation, because, as the author explains, tuning is a cumulative and progressive process. Much of what is said about the later, more powerful models assumes that the modifications pioneered with the basic 850 are taken into account. Technical changes incorporated in the Mini range after about the first ten years of production are not covered, and in some cases they may make what is suggested here unnecessary, as well as affecting questions of interchangeability. Remember too that Trickey's passion was racing, so that when he writes about the fragility of some engine components he often, though not always, means they tended to break at the astronomical revs employed to extract the last fraction of bhp: in less demanding circumstances the problems may well be much less acute.

There are some important principles which apply as much to tuning a Mini as any other car. It is a waste of time and money to attempt to tune a worn engine: any basic problems like bore or bearing wear must be eliminated first, and using, for example, a well worn oil pump is likely to be a false economy. With an older car, it is anyway often both practical and cost-effective to combine tuning and reconditioning. If you increase the power output and consequently the performance of any car, it is essential to ensure that the brakes, suspension and tyres are really up to it. And, particularly as we are dealing here with cars some of which will have endured the best part of three decades of Britain's rust-promoting climate, it is vital to be sure that the bodyshell is structurally sound.

In Clive Trickey's day, emission controls were just a distant rumour, and even now checks on the pollution from individual cars are still on the horizon and not yet a reality in the UK. But the situation has been much more closely controlled for a long time in many other countries. By improving the efficiency of an engine, performance tuning may in fact make it cleaner: alternatively it can sometimes have the reverse effect. In carrying out modifications to any car engine, it is important to pay due regard to any emission control regulations which may be in force in your country or state. In this respect the Mini, of course, is a good, socially responsible choice by virtue of its small engine size.

Small the engine may be, in relative terms, even in a Cooper S, but the Mini certainly makes good use of it. Other sporty cars have come and gone since the Mini first appeared, but few have been able to match the particular blend of fun and practicality which it offers. What these pages can provide is the opportunity to enhance that fun factor and the satisfaction that can be derived from developing, refining and improving the car by your own efforts.

Clive Trickey at full chat in his celebrated 850 Mini racer, KTR 223E.

8

1

Early Mini history

Throughout the evolution of the Mini there has been a continual sequence of modifications and improvements covering all aspects of the vehicle, sometimes involving the production of separate and distinct versions like the Cooper. This chapter deals with the technical changes in the early years.

1959 saw the introduction of the Mini in the first, rather crude 848cc form. It aroused both approving comment for the technical brilliance of the design and frequent criticism because it just would not keep water out and it had one of the worst gearboxes and most inefficient sets of brakes ever contrived. The roadholding was, and still is, phenomenal.

Even the average driver found that, after a few months' use, the synchromesh ceased to operate and, after several hard applications, the brakes became useless at speed. The excellent roadholding characteristics soon disappeared with the often rapid and complete failure of the standard shock absorbers, heralded normally by the most fearsome noises in the suspension department. This fault pursued the Mini right up till 1964, and even after that, until Hydrolastic suspension came on the scene, enthusiastic owners were invariably forced to fit special competition shock absorbers to overcome the problem completely.

After only a few months, a small improvement was made to the brakes by altering the size of the wheel cylinders at the rear. Also, the gearlever was cranked to improve the action and make it easier to reach.

The first Mini engine tuners found the crankshaft very short-lived, the timing gear and clutch even shorter-lived. Taking the latter fault first, this was found to result not from clutch weakness (especially when modded as described later) but from the existence of an oilway beneath the primary gear which allowed engine oil to find its way onto the clutch or from failure of an oil seal at the back of the crankshaft which would spin in its housing and let oil through. This seal was later modified and the oilway closed, thus curing the trouble. Until cranks without the oilway were produced, it was common practice to arc-weld the hole over, or fit a restrictor, but this often caused failure at the clutch end of the crank.

For a long time, nothing was done to improve the 848cc Mini timing gear and the only answer was to fit parts from another model. This timing gear fragility was, to a certain extent, tied up with crankshaft life. The sequence of events leading to failure was as follows: firstly, above 6,000rpm, the timing-chain tensioner would simply disintegrate; then, at 6,500rpm, the crankshaft set up a periodic vibration and started to whip, stretching the chain and breaking it in a matter of minutes. Also it was not uncommon for the timing wheels to break.

At first, the only remedy was to fit special steel timing wheels and frequently replace the timing chain (one for practice and one for the event when racing) though this normally meant doing without a tensioner. Later it was possible to obtain timing wheels to which double chains could be fitted, though they were scarce.

Minis coming down the production line at Longbridge in the early days. These examples have the Austin-style grille, and the model being built on the neighbouring line is the Austin A40, also powered by the A-series engine (though a conventional rear-drive design, of course).

The crankshaft vibration and whip, hardly surprisingly, also caused early failure of the shaft itself (and still does to some extent on ordinary Minis), breakage usually occurring at either of the end main bearings. Another problem was that, since the camshaft ran directly in the block without white-metal bearings, it could seize and cause a wrecked engine: the cure was to line-bore the block and fit bearings.

When the earliest pattern fuel pump was replaced by a type with higher output, the result was continual flooding because the needle valve in the carburettor was not man enough to cope with the increased pressure. This early type of carburettor was recognizable by the all-metal float and separate level-control arm.

One early feature which, although noisy, was not a weakness but in fact better than its later, quieter counterpart, was the four-bladed fan, cut down for competition to two-bladed form since it absorbed less power that way and was more efficient at high speeds. These became scarce but were a worthwhile acquisition for anything other than, say, a Cooper S, though only homologated for use on the 848cc Mini.

One other thing that always has been and still does prove a curse on Minis is the throttle cable. When hot, it expands and pinches the inner wire, making it difficult to obtain smooth throttle operation and preventing a slow tick-over.

A fault still common to all Minis is that the flywheel comes loose in constant use at high revs, and only careful assembly can minimize this tendency. The same is true of the crankshaft

pulley on all those models where it doubles as a vibration damper.

For a while, all Minis suffered from excessive engine rocking because of inefficient top engine mounts. The cure was to fit the steady bar with cones supplied for a few shillings by several accessory manufacturers, something that was not necessary later as the fault was cured in manufacture.

The first Mini road-wheels were too thin and cracked up under stress. That was soon put right by using thicker-gauge metal (the latter wheels being identified by 11 stamped on them) after a particularly embarrassing race meeting when, on making their first racing appearance, all the Minis proceeded to shed wheels all round the circuit and had to be quickly withdrawn.

The rockers on most Minis from about 1960 were made of pressed steel instead of cast and so were not suitable for lightening. Also, when using stronger valve springs and high-lift cams, the collets had a habit of cutting through the valve stem unless seated on a piece of steel shim.

A weakness of all the BMC A-series engines other than the Cooper S was a tendency for the centre main-bearing cap to break. Enthusiasts remedied this by fitting steel strengthening straps.

1961 saw the introduction of the long-stroke Cooper of 997cc capacity. It came, amid much publicity and ballyhoo, complete with twin HS2 carbs, free-flow exhaust manifold, high-lift camshaft and 'Formula Junior' crankshaft with torsional vibration damper. This, plus the promise of new-found stopping power through disc brakes

This is a 1959 Austin Seven: that was what the marketing men tried to call it, but the public would have none of it and adopted 'Mini' from the companion Morris Mini Minor. BMC had to agree, though separate Austin and Morris versions persisted for some time.

at the front, heralded a new era in Mini motoring. It represented a new approach from a British manufacturer in linking a famous racing name with its own and offering what amounted to an already converted car direct to the public with full works warranty and service back-up.

However, although very lively in performance, this version of the Mini turned out to be even more difficult to stop than its smaller-engined brother, the front discs being far too small and worse than useless. Few modifications gave any useful improvement, though many were tried: a later modification which entailed fitting larger calipers did help a bit.

The timing-chain tensioner still disintegrated at high revs, but the crankshaft damper cut out the whip in the shaft and stopped chain and sprocket breakages. The fact that the crankshaft had thicker webs and an enlarged tail end also increased its reliability.

The biggest single weakness with the engine were the clamp bolts which fastened the connecting rods to the gudgeon pins. These had a habit of breaking with consequent dire results. Some people had special rods with fully-floating pins made to counteract this, or else used rods from another engine: sometimes this can be done with little modification.

Early versions of this model had the oilway under the primary gear, and consequently tended to suffer from clutch slip. The gearbox suffered the same synchromesh troubles as before,

although the ratios were rather closer. One advantage was the introduction of a remote gear-change linkage, so that the Cooper version did not jump out of gear on rough ground as did the ordinary Mini.

Also in 1961, the Riley Elf and Wolseley Hornet were introduced. Apart from bodywork and trim, they were mechanically identical to the ordinary 848cc Mini, except that they had larger drum brakes, many of which soon found their way onto the front of ordinary Minis, with consequent useful increases in braking power.

1961-62: the oilway under the primary gear was blocked. This cured the clutch troubles. The carburettors on ordinary Minis were fitted with different needle valves, the floats being made of nylon and integral with the level-control arm, and this stopped the persistent flooding.

1962. The first real improvement to the whole Mini range came for the 1962 Motor Show, when all BMC vehicles fitted with the A-series engine, Minis included, had their gearboxes modified to incorporate baulk-ring synchromesh. This almost completely eliminated the faults and transformed a previously awful box into a quite acceptable unit which became enjoyable to use.

1962-63. Although the introduction of the Morris and MG 1100 models had provided a convenient source of fully-floating connecting rods for Mini enthusiasts, it was not until the Riley Elf and Wolseley Hornet were fitted with a new 998cc power unit that a production Mini

The 998cc engine first appeared in the two 'booted Minis', the Wolseley Hornet like this one and its Riley Elf counterpart, but was soon available in the original-shape versions as well.

engine with fully-floating rods came into existence. This engine was much stronger than either the 848cc or the Cooper 997cc unit, although this was not generally realized at the time. The bore-stroke ratio was much higher than on the 997cc design, and, with the fully-floating rods, this was an engine which just asked to be made to rev.

It was obviously only a matter of time before it would be fitted to the Cooper, complete with solid-skirt flat-top pistons, and this happened in 1964. The 998cc engine as fitted to the Cooper was otherwise similarly equipped to the old 997cc, with twin carburettors and crankshaft vibration damper, neither of which had featured on the Elf and Hornet version. This 998cc engine was quickly snapped up by all Cooper owners and many ordinary Mini owners too, as soon as its virtues were recognized.

By this time only the 848cc Mini still had the camshaft running directly in the block without white-metal bearings.

1963 saw a big step forward with the introduction of the Cooper S in 1,071cc, short-stroke form. This made even a Cooper fitted with the 998cc engine (a combination not in fact produced for another year) look positively archaic. Here at last was a Mini that stopped, with larger discs and rear drums, decent-sized calipers and servo assistance. The baulk-ring synchromesh gearbox now had needle-roller bearings instead of bronze-alloy bushes, and even closer ratios were an optional extra.

The engine, though basically similar in design, showed many departures from other BMC A-series units, some of them drawn from experience gained with the engine in Formula Junior single-seater racing. The whole unit was much strengthened throughout, including bearing housings and the block itself, in which the bore centres were differently spaced. The main-bearing journals were increased to 2in diameter, the clutch was enlarged and the timing gear was fitted with a double-row chain. The valves, beside being enlarged, were of special racing quality material and Stellite tipped. Special Hidural alloy valve guides were also used, and the rockers were cast, not pressed steel. The cylinder head was secured by eleven studs instead of the traditional nine. The gudgeon pins were much larger than on any other model and retained not by circlips but by an interference fit in the connecting rod.

The crankshaft was nitride-hardened in the interests of longer life at higher loadings. This must have been, and still is, one of the strongest engines ever to be mass-produced, and in its tuned form it was a credit to the overall design of the first 1959 Mini, for the suspension had remained basically the same.

The drive-shafts on the Cooper S were of much larger diameter, and the front wheel bearings were of the Timken taper-roller variety. The wheels were extra strong and came in 3½in or 4½in rim widths. Many extras were homologated for this car to help make it competitive in international motorsport.

1963-64. The 848cc Mini had its crankshaft strengthened and became as strong as the Elf or Cooper 998cc engine: the new part was in fact of similar specification.

The old shock absorbers were replaced by a new 'spring-loaded' gas-filled type which proved a little better.

1964. This year saw the introduction of the

The Mini-Cooper as it first appeared in Mk1 form in 1961. The tie-up with the famous Cooper racing team was a new departure for BMC and it was with this model that the Mini's rise to fame in sporting circles really began.

998cc Cooper, and the 1071 S was joined by 970 S and 1275 S versions, identical apart from engine capacity. All S models now had a diaphragm-spring clutch. Few S parts could be fitted to their lesser Mini brothers unless much modification was carried out: for example, it was impossible to fit S front brakes without also fitting S drive-shafts, wheels and so on.

The 1275 S engine was obviously the ultimate production version and attracted much of the tuners' attention. The only weakness was a tendency to shear the drive lug on the rotor arm, a result it seems of vibrations transmitted through the engine at certain revs. Tuners also found that the shell bearings soon wore out and the engine was difficult to keep cool.

In September 1964, all Minis other than estates and commercial types changed to Hydrolastic suspension. Diaphragm-spring clutches and gearboxes with needle-roller bearings, similar to those already used on the Cooper S, became standard across the range. As will be seen from the following tuning details for the 848cc Mini, many of the modifications recommended for early models were later incorporated in the more refined standard production versions.

In September 1965, automatic Minis and 1100s were announced. I will say no more about the transmission other than that it was revolutionary and cheap. However, since this transmission absorbed about 4bhp more than the manual type, it became necessary to increase the power output on automatic vehicles by an equivalent amount, and this opened up a new source of 'goodies' for the do-it-yourself tuner. Although small improvements were made to the cylinder head, that was not really of much interest because it was still a better bet to use a Cooper or MG 1100 head if you wanted to replace the one on a normal Mini. The really useful things were the the new inlet and exhaust manifold unit and the special 1½in HS4 SU carburettor which were used.

January 1967. The Cooper S received a few detail improvements aimed at increasing the reliability factor under competition conditions. The cylinder block was strengthened in the region of the main-bearing housings. Though I have never heard of an S block breaking or distorting, presumably the problem must have arisen, probably when the more powerful fuel-injected 8-port competition engine was being developed.

More important were the revised drillings in the crankshaft. Limited bearing life had always proved something of a problem on highly tuned Minis (mains on non-S and big-ends and mains on S). Now, however, the crankshaft had been cross-drilled to improve the oil feed to the bearings and extend their life.

In September 1967, the 998cc engine, in the 'cooking' version like that of the Hornet and Elf, became an option on most Mini saloons and estates, complete with the remote gear-change. Bodywork was revised, with a larger rear window and minor trim changes.

2

Tuning procedure

The tuning process described in this book is fundamentally a progressive one. In modifying the BMC A-series engine, and the Mini in particular, one starts off at an elementary stage, as typified by an early 850 Mini, and endeavours to achieve an ideal as fulfilled, with a few exceptions, by the Cooper S. Where there are elements of that ideal which for one reason or another cannot be achieved with, say, an 850 Mini – for example, square port shapes, which cannot be created without breaking through the head casting – they are explained, and they can be incorporated in the other versions, including the Cooper S. At each stage, the modifications are generally applicable either to a car which left the manufacturer in that state of tune or to a lesser model which has already been developed to that level: so a modified Cooper 998 is the same as a modified 998 Riley Elf or Wolseley Hornet, the latter being brought up to Cooper specification. In all versions and at all stages, elementary work such as balancing and matching of ports to manifolds is taken for granted.

Since many parts are interchangeable throughout the Mini range, cash will ultimately be the factor that limits the proximity of a modified 850's specification to that of a Cooper S. Note however that few of the S engine, gearbox, drive assembly or front suspension parts are individually interchangeable with most of the other, non-S versions: mostly they will have to be treated as complete assemblies. Some parts, though, can be adapted, and these are mentioned where applicable in the following chapters.

This book assumes a reasonable prior knowledge of the BMC Mini and is aimed at the more competent amateur enthusiast, mechanic and engine tuner. But any reasonably intelligent person, after a few hours browsing round a Mini and the appropriate handbook or manual, should be able to digest the following pages. What is done at manufacture, and what needs to be done, is mostly readily apparent. The chapters on specific aspects of tuning should be read in conjunction with the more general material on model changes over the years. There seems little point in quoting the details of the standard specification, bore and stroke, brake sizes, etc, because they have so often been published elsewhere.

I do not intend to delve into the realms of various conversion kits and proprietary tuning packages as their numbers are legion and their efficiency very varied. Nor is it for me to say which are of any use and which are not, though naturally I have my own ideas. Suffice to say that a firm's competition record is its best advert.

What I will do is to explain the various stages in principle and general design. These pages are not meant to be the last word. The man who implements these ideas along with a few of his own and a lot of trial-and-error work is the one who will find the few extra bhp and fractions of a second off acceleration times – or a few extra mpg, for an engine properly tuned for road use is usually more economical, through increased efficiency, than the standard unit.

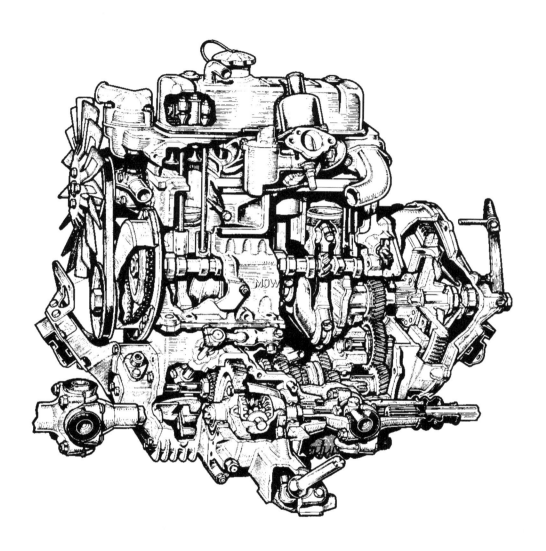

Cutaway drawing reveals details of the basic 848cc Mini engine and transmission assembly, including the transfer gears from crankshaft to gearbox and the clutch which is 'inside out' compared with that of a conventional rear-drive car.

Modifications to an engine are carried out basically in order to get more petrol-air mixture into the cylinders in a given time, then to burn as much of this mixture as possible, and finally to get the burnt residue out of the cylinders as efficiently as possible. I do not intend to dwell for long on the design aspects of inlet and exhaust systems or camshafts, because they are the subjects of several volumes in themselves. On the other hand, it would pay any really keen enthusiast to read at least some of what is available, and a good motoring book stockist will readily supply a list of titles.

It is the intention of this book to explain in reasonable detail how the average enthusiast with fairly limited knowledge can carry out his own conversion to his own motor car at a minimal cost. Although the main text deals with BMC Minis, much of it applies to other models powered by the A-series engine, in both transverse and in-line applications, and the same principles and techniques can be applied to many other types of vehicle, often with equally good results. I do think, though, that the Mini responds better to simple cylinder-head modifications than many other cars.

Equipment

Although it has been said that one can modify an engine using only hand tools, such as files and scrapers, I think that an electric drill is absolutely essential, not only because it speeds up the rate of work but also because there are certain operations that can only be done properly with this tool. Look for the best quality drill possible, with a 5/16in chuck and a minimum speed of about 1,400rpm. A good flexible shaft and a supply of rotary files and grinding stones of various shapes are the other essentials, together with the safety goggles which should always be worn when using such equipment. A small rubber disc (about 1¼in diameter) to which one can stick emery cloth is also very useful when trying to polish a flat surface. For other polishing jobs one needs a 4in rod with a slot cut in one end to hold an abrasive strip wrapped around it. Sometimes a piece of heater hose wrapped with emery cloth can serve the same purpose. I find that the greater the number and variety of tools available, the easier it is to do the job properly. A selection of small hand files is useful at times, though I always prefer to use rotary grinding stones where possible, since they not only tend to give a better finish but also work much more quickly.

Cylinder head work

Both the design and the finish of a mass-production cylinder head are the result of a compromise between what the designer would ideally like to see, the requirements of ordinary, everyday motoring for which most of the engines will be used, and the need to control manufacturing costs within tight limits. Consequently it is an area where many engines, and the BMC A-series is no exception, can be considerably improved, from the point of view of the enthusiast, by spending the time and/or money which the original maker cannot afford. Many people approach this phase of modification by buying an exchange head from a tuning company, and in this case one can only repeat the advice about sticking to firms with a good reputation and a proven record.

For the amateur who is willing to have a go at the job, though, a great deal can be achieved on a do-it-yourself basis, with the benefits of much lower costs and considerable satisfaction at the end of the day. This book will provide some basic guidance, but for anyone really interested more detailed information can be found elsewhere.

To promote better gas flow into and out of the cylinders, ports can be relieved, reshaped and sometimes enlarged, and the same goes for the combustion chambers, whilst valve diameters can be increased and compression ratios raised to the practical limits. When fitting larger valves the space available must be the ultimate governing factor. Although careful relieving of the chamber around the valve can increase the space to a certain extent, the gap around the valve should never be less than 1/16in, otherwise masking will occur, negating any benefit from the larger valve. Larger valves will also call for an increase in valve throat diameter by a proportionate amount. Exhaust valves do not need to be larger than nine-tenths of the size of the inlet valves, and eight-tenths is more than adequate.

The combustion chamber should be free of nooks and crannies in which unburnt vapour can collect, and the shape should be such as to keep the vapour moving so that it does not settle and condense out on the cooler walls. One aim is to produce vapour turbulence in the chamber and this is aided by the squish area opposite the spark plug, which also directs the fuel vapour towards the plug. Any work in the combustion chamber should always be finished by matching the volumes of the chambers using a burette and a paraffin-oil mixture. When working in the head,

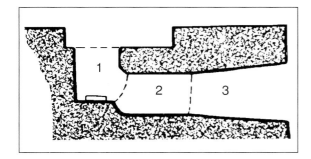

The inlet port can be seen as having a number of zones and it is important that modification does not drastically alter the ratio of their volumes one to another. The cross-section of the passage should not change abruptly in area.

damage to valve seats can be avoided by fitting old valves as blanking pieces.

Port shape also helps to promote turbulence and for this reason it is often better to have a curved port rather than a dead straight lead up to the valve throat. With the inlet tract, the amount of metal removed from the valve seat, guide and guide boss is determined largely by the immediate effect on gas flow and hence performance. But the governing factor in the case of the exhaust tract is heat transference: here, one should never remove much metal, if any, as the operating temperatures are far higher. Removal of metal will decrease the area over which heat dissipation can take place, leading to localized overheating, pre-ignition and, at worst, exhaust valve seizure or distortion.

In the inlet tract, worthwhile improvements are gained by removing the valve guide boss and removing or streamlining that part of the valve guide that projects into the port. The value of removing the valve guide projection depends in part on the particular engine and the purpose for which it is intended, since it does have the detrimental effect of increasing guide wear, and it can also reduce combustion chamber turbulence to a point where performance is impaired. If the guide remains, its thickness should at no point be less than $\frac{1}{16}$ in, but the projecting part can be shaped like a pencil point.

It is important to consider the port as a whole (no pun intended!) and remember that one cannot just alter one section and not another. Any modification must not greatly alter the dimensional relationship between one zone and another. This is because abrupt changes in the cross-sectional area of the port will be detrimental to good gas flow however smooth the walls may be.

Valves and seats

With standard heads, it is quite often the case that the valves are too wide so that the edges overhang into the chambers: this obstructs flow and, especially on the exhaust valves, can cause overheating and distortion. One can increase the valve throat size to $\frac{1}{8}$ in smaller than the overall diameter, which also increases the throat area by about 10%. On the other hand, one can achieve similar results by decreasing the valve size. With either method, care must be taken not to remove too much metal otherwise the valve will not locate properly when hot and may even pull right through the seat.

On some engines, reducing the angle of the seat and the seating area on the inlet valve to 30 degrees may be advantageous, but this is not advised for exhaust valves. The high operating temperatures reached by exhaust valves often cause flexing, and the standard 45-degree seating provides better location than the shallower angle.

The valves should be polished top and bottom, and inlet valves can be reshaped or, better still, improved-shape valves can be purchased. The tulip shape used for inlet valves on some engines with downdraught ports is not suitable for pushrod engines like the A-series because of the right-angle bend in the port and because some seat masking is unavoidable. The thin head 'penny-on-a-stick' shape is much more appropriate.

Compression ratio

The effects of improved breathing are usually enhanced by raising the compression ratio. Machining of the cylinder head should be undertaken with due consideration of the deck thickness, as a deck that is too thin will cause gaskets to blow.

Compression ratios are calculated using the accompanying formulae which will enable the desired combustion chamber volume to be determined. If that volume of paraffin-oil mixture is then run into the chamber with a burette, measuring the distance from the 'high water mark' to the head face will then indicate how much should be machined off the head, providing it is practical. The safe limit can often be ascertained by consulting others who have modified similar heads. Production castings vary one from another, though, and it is sometimes possible to shave more from one than from an apparently similar equivalent.

Removal of metal from the combustion chambers of course lowers the compression ratio,

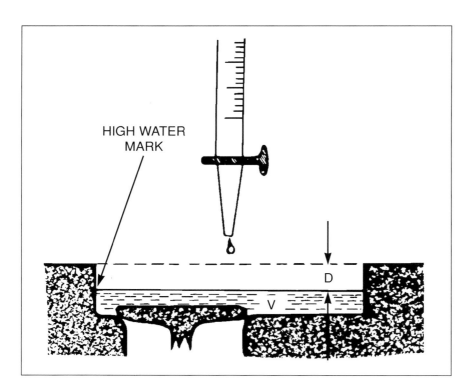

HIGH WATER
MARK

D

V

Combustion chamber volume is measured by running a paraffin-oil mixture into the chamber from a burette: before and after readings from the burette scale give the volume. This technique is used both to check that the modified chambers have equal, matching volumes and to determine the amount to be skimmed from the head to achieve the desired compression ratio, dimension D in this (exaggerated) example.

but this may be a necessary evil if one is endeavouring to reduce valve masking, improve gas flow and ignition characteristics or match chamber volumes.

After machining, any frazes or ragged edges around oilways, waterways or combustion chambers should be removed as they can cause gasket sealing problems.

Valve gear improvements

The removal of weight in the valve operating mechanism is very important, since every moving ounce requires perhaps 20 to 30 pounds of valve spring pressure to prevent valve bounce. Thus any weight reduction can permit the use of lighter springs, causing less stress and wear, or conversely enabling the engine to run at higher revs on a given type of spring.

The most obvious target for weight reduction is the rockers. The pressed steel pattern cannot be lightened to any extent and should be replaced by cast rockers where possible – for example replace those of the 997 Cooper with the type fitted to the A40. Remove metal at the valve end down to the area that touches the valve. The adjuster end can be thinned down to leave 0.080in (80 thou) of metal outside the thread and the boss can be reduced in height. This may enable the adjuster

screws to be shortened, and one can also use smaller nuts. Generally the shank should be left alone except for polishing to remove the roughness at the edges. More details in Chapter 16.

The distance springs between rockers should be replaced by tubular phosphor bronze bushes in order to remove the resistance imparted by the springs. This also enables one to centralize the rockers more accurately over the valves. End-float of the rockers on the rocker shaft should be about 0.002in (2 thou).

The solid steel pushrods can be replaced by the high-tensile tubular variety, but I do not like aluminium-alloy pushrods because they have too great a variation in length due to expansion when they get hot. When using tube, the solid ends of the original pushrods can be cut off and pushed into the tube, and then these solid ends can be ground away to minimum size. It is sometimes possible to use lightweight motorcycle pushrods in a car engine if you can find some of suitable dimensions.

The face of the rocker which contacts the tip of the valve stem should be radiused so that it is always effectively at right-angles to the stem, whatever the stage of opening of the valve. Any variation will impart a sideways load to the valve, causing excessive valve guide wear, and

Formulae for capacity and compression ratio

D = cylinder bore
S = stroke
CR = compression ratio
V = swept volume of one cylinder
vc = total engine capacity
n = number of cylinders
H = volume of chamber in cylinder head
A = volume given by gasket thickness, piston crown shape, space above top ring, distance of piston from top of block at TDC, valve pockets if any, etc. Remember that pistons with raised crowns will reduce volume **A** whereas dished pistons will increase it. This volume can be measured by the burette method.

$$V = \frac{vc}{n} = \left(\frac{D}{2}\right)^2 \times 3.14 \times S$$

$$CR = \frac{V+H+A}{H+A}$$

$$H = \left(\frac{V+H+A}{CR}\right) - A$$

Thus if we know the values for any three of the factors **H**, **V**, **CR** and **A**, we can find the unknown fourth factor by substituting into the formulae. Take two examples:

1: If volume of one cylinder is 250cc, combustion chamber volume in the head is 21cc and additional volume **A** is 6cc, to calculate the compression ratio:

$$CR = \frac{V+H+A}{H+A} = \frac{250+21+6}{21+6} = \frac{277}{27}$$

$$\therefore CR = 10.26:1$$

2: If we want a compression ratio of 10:1, V = 250 and A = 6 as before, to calculate the required volume of the chamber in the head:

$$CR = \frac{V+H+A}{H+A} = 10 = \frac{250+H+6}{H+6}$$

$$\therefore 10H+60 = 256+H$$
$$\therefore 9H = 196 \qquad \therefore H = \frac{186}{9}$$
$$\therefore H = 21.77cc$$

encouraging flexing and ultimate failure of the valve stem itself.

If valves have been ground-in a long way, it may be necessary to remove metal from the valve stem tip to avoid extreme rocker angles. Alternatively, if the cylinder head face has been drastically machined, one may have to raise the level of the rocker-shaft pedestals with packing shims for the same reason: another method is to fit shorter pushrods.

The cam followers can usually be extensively lightened by boring them out, thus giving a thinner wall to the barrel, and radiusing the top edges. Finally, when using an extreme camshaft and very strong valve springs, it may be necessary to replace the spring retaining collars with special machined steel items. In many cases the oil shield cups attached to the collars can be dispensed with.

Camshaft

The camshaft specification is one of the major factors which determines the characteristics of the engine. The type of camshaft chosen depends upon the use to which the vehicle is to be put. It is no use using a full-race cam on a shopping car, as it will be most intractable. On the other hand, for racing one is not worried about tractability, maximum power is the important thing.

It should be pointed out that changing the camshaft must go hand-in-hand with other modifications. A really wild camshaft will seldom give good results unless the inlet and exhaust manifolds are of efficient design. An exhaust manifold with only short, linked pipes will probably cause spitting back through the carbs even at high revs when used in conjunction with an extreme camshaft.

The design and production of camshafts is a complex and specialized business best left to the experts, whose advice is readily available through the better tuning firms. For popular cars like the Mini, a wide variety of alternative camshafts is available and the question of choosing the most suitable for a particular engine and a particular use is covered in more detail in Chapter 15.

A point worth watching is that some standard engines have the camshaft running direct in the block, without liner bearings. When fitting a different cam it is strongly recommended – and essential for competition engines – that bearings are fitted, after first line-boring the block to accept the liners. This can be carried out quite cheaply by most machine shops and is really not a do-it-yourself job.

Ignition

When an engine is modified it is almost always necessary to alter the ignition timing as well as the fuel mixture in order to obtain the best results. When using the standard distributor, it is a good idea to disconnect the vacuum advance and retard mechanism to prevent engine failure caused by over-advance at high revs.

If a non-standard camshaft is to be fitted, one should either buy a new distributor with the advance curve matched to the characteristics of the cam, or obtain a modified version from the camshaft designer or supplier: on an exchange basis this is fairly inexpensive. If a BL camshaft from a different model is to be used, the existing distributor can often be modified to suit: more details in Chapter 18.

Carburettor modifications

An increase in choke size, or at least a change of jets or needles, is usually necessary to take full advantage of other tuning modifications. Careful polishing of the choke tube to improve the carburettor's efficiency often makes worthwhile improvements. Increasing the size of the choke tube necessitates different jets to supply more fuel and prevent flat spots. It may alternatively be possible to use a larger carburettor or one of completely different type: this will almost

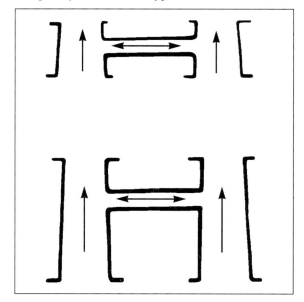

Basic layout of inlet manifolds for twin carburettors with short (top) and long ram pipes. The balance pipe between the two main passages is an essential feature.

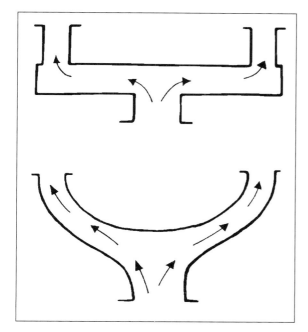

Two approaches to the design of a single-carburettor inlet manifold. Top is the standard Mini pattern, below a special free-flow design. Although apparently an obvious improvement, the latter type needs careful design to achieve any advantage over the ordinary 'log' type.

certainly make some manifold modifications essential. Best known, of course, is the use of multiple carburettors to replace a standard single unit – even granny knows what 'it's a twin-carb job' means!

Inlet manifold

The principles underlying the design and modification of inlet manifolds are closely similar to those for cylinder heads mentioned earlier. The starting point, of course, is the number and type of carburettors to be used. The object is to obtain as smooth and unobstructed a passage as possible from the atmosphere end of the carburettor into the combustion chamber, and modification follows much the same lines as for the ports in the head.

When choosing a manifold or designing a new one, remember that the length of the inlet tract from the carburettor to the valve heads is a very decisive governing factor for the torque and maximum power characteristics of an engine, and may involve the do-it-yourself enthusiast in much trial-and-error work.

In some cases it may pay to set the carbs and

manifold at an angle, say 30 degrees, to give a downward rake towards the cylinder head. Certainly, the 'semi-downdraught' layout had a long period of popularity.

The manifold should always be carefully matched to the ports, as any unintentional step at the joint face will negate all that careful work which went into getting a smooth internal profile.

Exhaust system design

The lengths and diameters of the various pipes and branches in the manifold and the rest of the exhaust system are very important when tuning an engine for optimum performance, especially when using a vigorous camshaft. If an exhaust system is properly designed, offering as little resistance as possible to the flow of gas, then the motion of that gas down the pipe away from the cylinder not merely empties the combustion chamber efficiently but also helps to suck in the next charge of fresh fuel-air mixture.

With the short-branch exhaust manifold of the type often supplied in cast iron as a standard fitment, the exhaust gas can sometimes come down one branch and up the adjacent one, even entering the next cylinder, especially at low revs, with a camshaft which provides extra overlap. Thus the preferred design has long individual branches from each cylinder leading eventually into a common pipe.

Although increases in the exhaust pipe diameter towards the outlet end can help gas flow, too large an increase too soon can have the opposite effect, reducing gas velocity and impeding flow. It has often been claimed that a shorter main pipe improves bottom-end power when using a more extreme camshaft, but this is

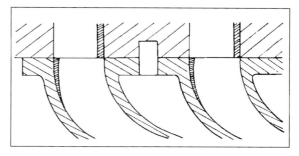

The openings of the inlet manifold should always be carefully matched to the ports in the cylinder head to eliminate any obstructions to flow. A paper pattern can be used to facilitate this operation. Remember that the gasket may need trimming too.

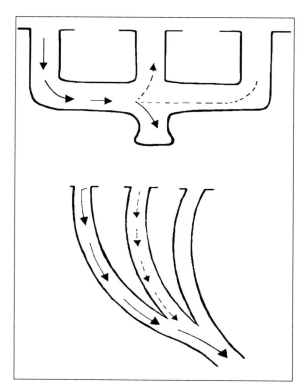

With an exhaust manifold of the standard pattern as fitted to the Mini (top) the gas flow from one port can sometimes interfere with that from the other ports, to the detriment of efficiency. In a well designed 'extractor' manifold (bottom) gas flowing from one port helps to suck residual gases from the other passages.

an over-simplification and not always true, especially with megaphones or expansion boxes.

I would always recommend that an enthusiast wanting to get the best from an engine and intending to use special manifolds should pick an established design from one of the reputable tuning shops: it is usually cheaper as well as easier in the long run. To deal in any more detail with manifold design would need a lot more explanation than there is room for here, but there are several good books on the topic for anyone wanting to delve more deeply. Like cylinder head design, it is a subject for which some people develop a strange fascination – sometimes to the point where the rest of the car gets completely neglected!

But it is important to remember again that tuning must maintain all the engine's systems in harmony, so any alterations to the exhaust will usually make mixture and timing adjustments essential.

Pistons

Split-skirt or T-slot pistons are common in production engines: although quiet in operation they are weaker than good solid-skirt competition pistons. The pistons should be as light as possible to reduce crankshaft bearing loads and strain on connecting rods, but adequate strength must not be sacrificed for lightness.

One should ensure that the gudgeon bosses are well supported by ribs, and the inner edges of the gudgeon bores should be rounded off to a radius of about $\frac{1}{16}$in. It is vital that the piston crown is thick enough for strength and to conduct away the great heat to which it is subjected.

The drain holes behind the oil-control rings should not be too numerous, otherwise the top of the piston may come off. The top ring should preferably be the L-section pressure-backed Dykes type. Ordinary 'iron' rings (as opposed to chrome rings) should not be run in.

Valve pockets in the piston (or block) should provide a clearance of at least 0.070in (70 thou) both from the valve face and around the diameter, and the edges should be nicely radiused. These pockets are cut into the top of the block or the piston crown directly beneath the valve. Their purpose is to prevent the valve, at full lift, from hitting the block or piston, and they are normally only necessary when using an extreme camshaft or much enlarged valves. There are also circumstances, though, when machining operations on the cylinder head reduce the clearance so much that pockets become necessary: the MGB and Austin/Morris 1800 are typical examples of engines where this can happen. Unfortunately one cannot give any hard-and-fast rules, only advise very careful measurement of clearances during assembly. Personally, I always halve any clearance measurements to allow for the settling down of the engine after a few hours' running and the consequent re-tightening of various nuts and bolts.

Block and bottom end

The face of the cylinder block should be resurfaced if necessary. One can bore the block oversize to increase capacity, but it is advisable to seek a precedent or accept the manufacturers' recommendations, since too large an increase in bore diameter may excessively weaken the block, or even make it porous. The availability of suitable pistons is, of course, one of the deciding factors.

Bearing cap bolts are often an engine's biggest weakness and they should always be replaced by

Club racing at Brands Hatch, 1960s-style: the Mini's dominance in the smaller-capacity saloon classes was almost complete.

high-quality new ones. Big-end and main-bearing shells should be replaced by heavy-duty alternatives, especially when considerable higher revs are to be used. Where any big increase in performance is the aim, the main bearing caps should be replaced by a high-quality steel variety, or at least be fitted with additional steel support straps. This may not always prove necessary, but is usually advisable on production engines. Complete replacement steel bearing caps need line-boring in situ to match the block, and are rarely interchangeable: support straps, however, are a quite effective substitute and usually are interchangeable.

Suitable straps can be made from ordinary mild steel reasonably easily, using simple hand tools plus preferably an electric drill and attachments. They consist of a main strap and spacer pieces set so as to leave pinch gaps of about 0.005in (5 thou). Extra long bearing-cap bolts are of course needed and must be properly made from a decent high-tensile steel. It is also necessary to machine

or file a flat on each of the standard bearing caps so that the support strap can be properly located.

The crankshaft and connecting rods should be checked for wear, straightness and truth, and then crack-tested. All imperfections and excessive roughness should be carefully removed, and the edges of all holes and oilways should be radiused. If possible, it is best to use a crankshaft which has large radiuses between the journals and webs. In most circumstances where considerable performance increases are envisaged, it is not advisable to use a reground crankshaft unless there is no alternative. Sometimes the manufacturers' competition department or one of the larger tuning shops can supply extra strong crankshafts and rods: these are really only required for competition use and tend to be expensive, but are always cheaper than a major blow-up.

It may be possible to fit a crankshaft vibration damper, but care should be taken to obtain one that has the correct frequency. The clutch may be too weak in standard form, and either a

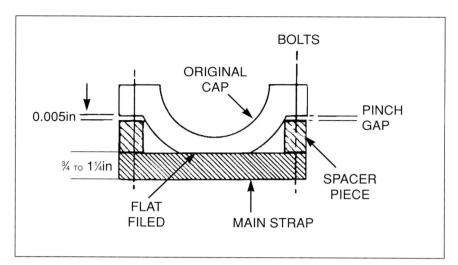

Mild-steel straps can be fitted to reinforce the main-bearing caps, secured with new, longer bolts. A flat is filed on the cap as a seating for the strap, and spacers are dimensioned to give a 0.005in pinch gap which is closed when the bolts are tightened.

competition pattern or a larger one should be fitted. Fretting often occurs between the flywheel and the crankshaft flange: this can be prevented by making sure that the dowels are a good tight fit or, better still, by increasing the number of fixing bolts. The flywheel can be carefully lightened (but not to the point where its strength is impaired: failure due to centrifugal force can be very nasty) or replaced by a lightweight steel one if available. This will not increase top speed but can improve throttle response and acceleration and will help to reduce torsional loads on the crankshaft. It can make a smooth tick-over difficult to obtain, but that won't worry the competition enthusiast.

The final stage in modifying a production engine should be careful balancing. Unlike most of the previous work, which a competent enthusiast can do himself (with the exception of crack testing), balancing should be left to the qualified experts who are the only ones able to do it: this is a few pounds well spent. Every moving part should, ideally, be balanced, though few people bother about accurate balancing of valve gear. Lightening the flywheel is usually carried out with balancing and, again, I would not advise the enthusiast to do this himself.

In conclusion

I cannot over-emphasize the need to check dimensions and clearances during assembly. It may at times be found that some machining is needed here and there in order to make things fit: this is due not only to production tolerances but also to changes in specifications and castings from model to model and sometimes from year to year.

For example, one may occasionally find on fitting pistons to different connecting rods that they either project above the block or are sunk below the top a little, so that either the tops of the pistons or the block should be machined off as applicable, providing the amount involved is not excessive. Perhaps a special connecting rod is a little too wide to fit onto a big-end journal, and needs to be carefully machined each side to reduce the width. Every component must be left with a sufficient reserve of strength, and you must remember that metal removed cannot be put back. Think each modification through before you embark on it. Common sense is the key: it is simply not possible for me to cover every combination and every peculiarity, but if you read right through the book you should be able to build up a set of general guide-lines. The final decisions have to be yours.

Two final words of warning to the would-be engine tuner. Firstly, before taking the vehicle out to see what it will do, make certain, by doing several plug tests, that the mixture is right or, at worst, too rich. Weak mixture causes holes in the tops of pistons, as also do spark plugs that are too soft. A fully tuned race engine needs racing plugs if the full performance is to be used. When carrying out a plug test, never let the engine idle, not even just before switching the ignition off: always switch off at peak revs and always carry out the test on a hot engine. Secondly, always make sure that the ignition timing is somewhere near correct right through the rev range and not just at idling speed or with the engine static before using sustained high revs. Wrong timing in such circumstances quickly produces wrecked engines.

24

3

850 stage 1 and 2 tuning

Stage one engine tuning consists of carrying out all the basic work on the cylinder head which is essential in any further tuning of a Mini. This basically involves raising the compression ratio by machining the cylinder head face, and carefully reshaping the combustion chambers and ports to improve the gas flow, thereby gaining better filling of each cylinder.

One should be very careful when having the Mini cylinder head machined as the maximum amount that it is safe to remove is about 0.070 to 0.080in (70 to 80 thou). Beyond that, one is liable to break through into the oilway which runs parallel with the head face at a depth which varies from one casting to another. Fortunately, its position can be accurately determined with a depth gauge to decide exactly how much to machine from each particular head. Using standard pistons and with proper combustion chamber modifications, this should give a compression ratio of about 9.5:1.

Turning now to the gas-flowing of the combustion chambers and ports, care is once again required with this particular engine as it is quite possible to break through into the water jacket or pushrod holes if too much metal is removed. Also remember that the removal of any metal from the combustion chamber lowers the compression ratio, although this is the lesser of two evils up to a certain point and it is necessary to strike a compromise. It is difficult to get the chamber volume below 19cc.

It was possible at one time to obtain special rough-cast cylinder heads, from BMC or Downton Engineering, which had more metal in the areas where modifications are desirable, allowing the achievement of higher compression ratios and more complete gas-flowing of the ports without fear of breaking into water or oil passages.

In the combustion chambers, metal should be removed as shown in the drawing, with particular emphasis on the area round the inlet valve, the object being to reduce masking by the chamber wall and projecting beak. The edges of the chamber can be rounded off as shown but one must use a special gasket of the type made for the Cooper or 948cc Sprite Mk2 (BMC part number 12A190). Care must be taken not to remove too much metal from between the chambers or gasket sealing troubles will develop. Around the spark plug hole, it is only necessary to remove the sharp edge: too much metal removed can cause pocketing and expose the plug threads to excessive temperatures, as well as lowering the compression ratio.

Probably the most important modifications to the cylinder head are carried out in the inlet tracts – ports, valve throats, valves and seats. The aim is to make the passage from the carburettor into the combustion chamber as free and smooth as possible. Like most other do-it-yourself enthusiasts, I do not have access to a dynamometer or a flow bench, so I have always worked on the basis of being able to look into the port from the manifold end and see out through the valve throat into the combustion chamber.

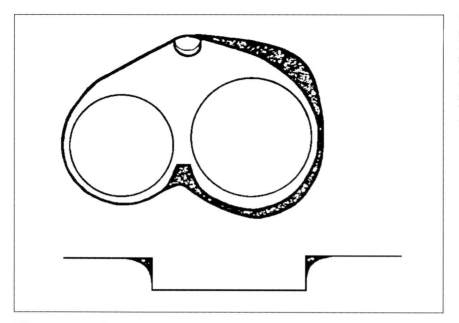

Gas flowing Mini 850 combustion chamber. Remove metal from shaded areas, rounding off chamber edges around the inlet valve as shown in lower section. Take care not to undercut the gasket area.

The amount of daylight that can be seen also serves as a useful guide when balancing the volumes of the ports and throats.

The diagrams show the original shape and the shape to be aimed at. One should remove the inlet valve guide boss, but on no account shorten the valve guide since doing so not only increases wear but reduces combustion chamber turbulence to the detriment of power. But the part of the guide which projects into the port can be tapered off, like sharpening a pencil, for the best result. The valve throat area, between the guide and the valve seat, should be given a rounded finish and if possible be nicely cup-shaped, somewhat like an egg cup, rather than tending to be angular and having a flat base at the valve guide boss. Unless you are fitting larger valves, though, the throat diameter beneath the valve seat must not be bored out in an attempt to increase the effective valve area, because this ruins gas-flow characteristics and results in an engine with poor torque.

The inlet valve seat can be made into a complete curve, as also can the valve seating face. The latter can be done using a low-speed drill, with the valve mounted in the drill chuck, and a fairly coarse hand file. A final finish is given by using the same drill, or better still a high-speed one, and fine emery cloth. The valve seat should be carefully rounded off using a small, fine hand file and various grades of emery cloth. Take care only to remove the sharp edges of the seat, without enlarging the diameter measured across

the mid-point between throat and combustion chamber. Then carefully reseat the valve using valve grinding paste to produce a pencil-line seat. This gives ideal gas-flow conditions and is completely reliable.

The projection at the bifurcation of the port should be tapered back a little. On no account should it be left with a sharp edge, but should form a gradual curve. Where the port passes between the pushrod holes, great care must be taken that the width does not exceed one inch, to avoid breaking through. Very good results can be obtained simply by streamlining this part of the port, with no significant increase in width, particularly if one is aiming at high-torque characteristics.

It is a good idea to make templates of the port cross-section shapes from thin sheet material. This helps to achieve accuracy of size and shape, and makes matching the ports one to another much easier. Looking into the port from the manifold face, the ideal cross-section for the area beyond the pushrod position and before the port divides is as close as possible to square, though this cannot be fully realized. Heads for other versions of the BMC A-series engine have this shape in the original casting, as detailed later.

Little work is necessary in the exhaust ports, but if you have plenty of time you can smooth them along the same lines as the inlet ports, remembering that they must be matched to the manifold. But it is vital that metal is not removed

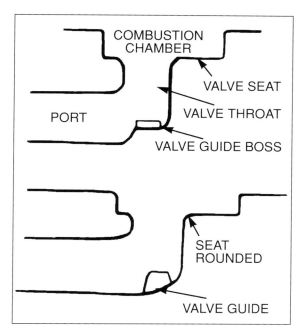

Cross-sections of standard (top) and modified (below) inlet valve seat, throat and port. The boss surrounding the valve guide projection is smoothed away and the valve seat is blended into a continuous radius.

from the valve, valve seat, valve guide or guide boss: any reduction in the amount of metal at these points reduces the area over which heat can be conducted away from the hot exhaust valve, with the consequent danger that the valve will overheat and seize or distort. However, it is safe to remove a small amount of metal from the inside of the curve opposite the guide boss, as illustrated. A useful guide to the amount to remove is that one should be able to push one's index finger (a little under ¾in thick) comfortably without a squeeze down past the valve seat and round the bend into the straight part of the port. The port so modified gives adequate gas flow.

Valves springs are partly a matter of choice and availability. With most 848cc engines which have not been fully balanced, 5,500 to 6,500rpm is quite sufficient, unless engine life is of no great concern. So most commercially available 'extra strong' springs are quite suitable, and even standard single Sprite Mk2 or Cooper springs are strong enough. If the engine is for racing, then many tuning shops offer really strong race springs, either single or double. In conjunction with lightened valve gear, these will allow 8,000rpm, but such revs are not to be

recommended for the ordinary user who wants a fast, reliable road car.

When fitting stronger springs, the collets must be seated on steel shims, otherwise they may gradually cut through the valve stem and cause the valve to drop into the engine. These shims fit around the valve stem, in the collet groove, like a collar. The collets then seat on the shims which act as a buffer between collet and valve stem. Shims can easily be cut from steel foil 0.002 or 0.003in thick, using scissors.

Manifold and carburettor

It is possible to get very good results from the 850 Mini simply by modifying the cylinder head as already detailed. However, in my opinion, for the little extra work involved it is well worth gas-flowing the inlet manifold and improving the carburettor efficiency. The inlet manifold should be carefully sawn off where it is joined to the exhaust manifold (they are manufactured as one unit). This removes the hot-spot and prevents premature 'frying' of the fuel mixture. It is easier to shape and polish the inlet manifold properly if it is first sawn into three pieces so that one has three relatively straight tubes to work on. Reshape the internal surfaces, aiming to make the passage from the carburettor to the cylinder head as straight and smooth as possible. Do not remove the rib that runs along the main trunk of the manifold. Finish off by giving a final polish and carefully weld the manifold back together again, taking care not to allow too much weld to run inside and defeat the object of the smoothing operations just carried out. If you are not too keen on cutting and re-welding the manifold, gas-flowing and

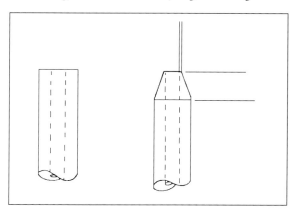

The inlet valve guide can be tapered (right) where it projects into the port, but it should not be shortened.

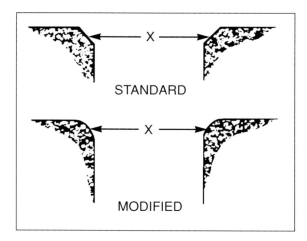

STANDARD

MODIFIED

The inlet valve seat can be blended into a continuous curve. Do not increase the diameter at the mid-point, X, where grinding the valve in lightly will create a pencil-line seating area.

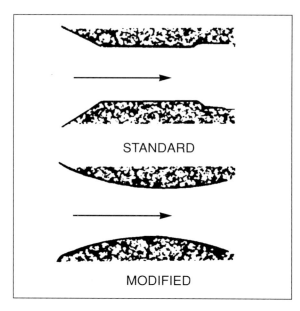

STANDARD

MODIFIED

The aim is to produce a continuous, smooth passage through the inlet port from manifold to valve throat.

smoothing just those parts that can be reached with suitable tools will give quite good results.

There is little point in doing much work on the standard exhaust manifold, beyond removing any really bad protuberances or rough areas in the casting and ensuring that it matches the cylinder head ports.

For most purposes, including road use and casual competition, the standard 1¼in HS2 SU carburettor is quite adequate. Ease of tuning makes it the best proposition, in the hands of an inexperienced enthusiast, unless one can afford to utilize the services of a carburation expert or spend a lot of time learning by trial and error. With this carburettor, do not remove the air filter case, although you can leave the element out at the expense of some extra noise and accelerated engine wear. The reason for not removing the filter case is that the HS2 has a very short choke tube and the additional trumpet and chamber help to obtain the necessary speed of flow by providing a ram effect.

The carburettor itself should be set up using a fast-lift vacuum chamber and piston assembly, obtainable from tuning specialists, complete with blue spring and E3 needle. The damper should be retained and very thin machine oil used in the dashpot. The overall effect seems to be to make an engine more lively and responsive, at the same time improving petrol consumption.

Some people have recommended complete removal of the piston damper, particularly as a competition modification, but I have never found this to be of any advantage even for top-end power and it is definitely a disadvantage at lower revs.

The complete dashpot assembly consists of the carburettor piston, spring, damper, needle and piston cover or chamber: the needle and spring can be changed for differently calibrated ones in the course of tuning, but the piston, damper and cover should be treated as a single unit because the parts are matched. Bits and pieces from one dashpot assembly must on no account be swapped for bits and pieces from another – this would be about as bad as fitting a part-worn big-end bearing from another car. So if you drop and break the piston cover, for example, it is no use going to the scrapyard for another: you must obtain a complete assembly.

The butterfly can be thinned down to a knife edge on the side facing towards the atmosphere when in the full-throttle position, but care must be taken not to impair its seating against the choke wall when in the closed position. The projections of the screws fixing the butterfly to the spindle should be carefully removed.

The carburettor choke tube and the alloy trumpet to which the filter case is attached can with advantage be carefully polished and matched up, and the carburettor should be accurately matched to the inlet manifold, not forgetting to include the gaskets and spacers in the matching operations.

Section through an inlet port looking down from the top. Shaded areas indicate where metal is removed to 'streamline' the passage. Because of the presence of the pushrod holes, P, the width at X must not exceed one inch. The cross-section at Y, circular in the head as manufactured, should be modified nearer to the ideal 'square' shape, S, but this ideal cannot be fully achieved in the ordinary 850 head casting.

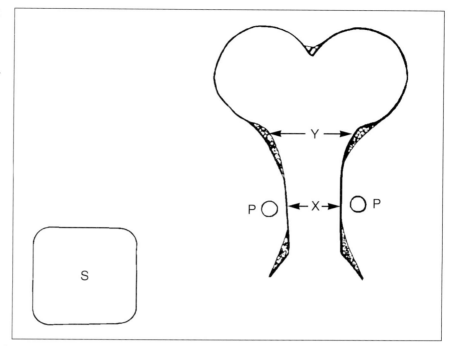

An effective and convenient heat shield can be made up from thin aluminium sheet and attached to the float chamber utilizing the screws which retain the float chamber lid. The shield should be shaped and bent so that it stays about half an inch clear of the float chamber in the vertical position and shields it from the exhaust manifold.

Exhaust system

Having got this far with the tuning procedure, it is advisable to fit a decent silencer of the straight-through variety. Probably the best and cheapest method I have found is to use a standard Austin-Healey Sprite Mk1 silencer. The exhaust pipe should be re-routed to emerge at the centre of the rear of the vehicle and not to one side as standard. This is most easily done by cutting the tail pipe just forward of the first bend after the straight run under the tunnel and welding about six or eight inches of straight pipe of similar specification in place. The silencer, with the standard bracket removed, can then be clamped over this and will emerge straight out at the rear. It is advisable to arrange an extra hanging strap just under the rear valance. If using any other type of silencer, make sure the exit pipe is larger than the inlet (the Sprite silencer is ideal in this respect). I personally would steer clear of any of the decorative twin-pipe silencers on the market for, in my opinion, they give no extra improvement in performance

and are very expensive.

At this stage, do not try to fit a larger diameter pipe all the way through from the manifold as, far from helping, this will slow the exhaust gases down to a point where a reduction in performance occurs.

Stage two

Stage two modifications mainly involve further developments of the carburation and cylinder head. One cannot expect to see as large a gain from these improvements as that achieved in going from standard to stage one. Some people may decide that they only want to further develop the carburation and not further modify the cylinder head. But, unless one is working within the constraints of a particular set of competition regulations, I think that there is little point in doing one without the other.

Regulations aside, the carburettor options are to fit a larger single SU (in this case the 1½in H4), or twin carburettors, or one twin-choke carburettor such as a Weber. For the moment, I am only going to deal with fitting a single SU H4, but I will cover twin-carb applications and special manifolds later. The carburettor itself should be modified along the lines already described for the SU HS2, but the final set-up – particularly the spring and needle type – in this case is even more dependent on trial and error to obtain optimum results. A good needle to start off with is the RO, but this is certainly not to be taken as the last word, since the more engines are modified the more they tend to vary one from another, even if the principles behind the modifications remain the same.

It is of course necessary to further modify the inlet manifold when fitting an SU H4. The mouth of the manifold must be opened up to match the 1½in choke tube of the carburettor. While it is quite satisfactory to do this by removing ⅛in all round the periphery of the opening, there is a way of gaining a little extra improvement. This involves removing the necessary metal from the top and upper sides only, so that in effect the centre of the new circular opening is offset upwards from the old centre. This will necessitate relocating the carburettor fixing studs, moving them up the manifold flange, and this should be carried out with great care, the old stud holes being welded up and the flange face resurfaced. The result is to raise the position of the carburettor relative to the manifold and ports, and this provides a slightly more straight-through induction tract and hence a small power bonus.

The SU H4 has a much longer choke tube than the HS2 so the air cleaner body is not required from an air-flow point of view. There may be some advantage to be gained by fitting a pukka carburettor intake trumpet, though I have personally never found it to be of any use in this particular case. If the time is available, it might be worth experimenting with trumpets of various lengths in the hope of hitting on the ideal, but remember that such work must invariably go hand-in-hand with further checking and adjustment of the mixture.

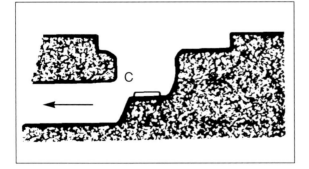

Section through exhaust port. Little if any metal must be removed, but some rounding at point C is permissible.

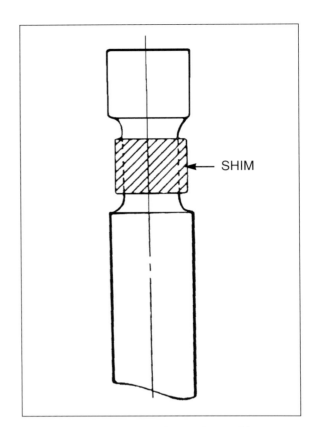

When fitting stronger valve springs, shims must be fitted around the valve stems, in the collet grooves, to provide a seating for the collets and prevent fretting which can lead to valve failure.

Though there may be some advantages in not fitting an air cleaner, it can be very dangerous because, when starting from cold, all carburettors have a tendency to spit back at times, and on a Mini this can fill the speedo housing aperture with petrol vapour. One spark, or a flame from the carb when it spits back, and up she goes – unless you move a trifle smartish, you're left with a cinder! I know, it happened to me, and I got blisters all over my hands and a ruined overcoat in putting the fire out before it completely destroyed the car. I still had to renew all the wiring and hoses under the bonnet.

After that, I fitted a flame shield to prevent it happening again. I made it from a simple pancake-type filter designed originally for the standard Cooper HS2 carburettor. I removed some of the wire filling, enlarged the flange hole and relocated the stud holes to make it fit my H4. The similar filter intended for a 1½in carb was not suitable as it effectively made it impossible to

Track testing a racing Cooper S for *Motor Racing* magazine in the early days before wide wheels became all the rage.

fit the speedo cable. The flame shield had no detectable adverse effect on the performance of my luke-warm Mini.

This problem does not arise if you use the complete HS4 carburettor assembly as fitted to Minis with automatic transmission. As already mentioned, the introduction of that version provided the enthusiast with an extra source of tuning goodies. Although the manifolds do not look much different from those fitted to manual-transmission Minis, they have proved to be a worthwhile improvement. Though it may take some swallowing, it is a fact that this simple cast-iron exhaust manifold gives better results than the more elaborate and better-looking Cooper long-branch steel manifold. The inlet manifold, of course, needs no modification to take a 1½in carburettor as it is intended for the HS4.

Modifications should follow the lines already detailed. Remove the air filter element but leave the case behind to act as a plenum chamber. Needless to say, a different needle will be required, and for a Mini with standard valves and camshaft, I suggest an AO needle as a starting point.

For anyone wanting a single-carburettor conversion, this assembly fitted complete to a modded head offers an inexpensive and very efficient modification. I personally would use it in preference to the standard Cooper or MG 1100 twin-carburettor set-up every time. Among other advantages over the earlier suggestion of using an H4 SU is the fact that one can retain a proper air filter and fully operational cold-start mechanism if required.

Unfortunately the manifold flange on the HS4

carburettor is different from those of the HS2 and H4, so it is not possible to fit an HS4 to a standard (manual) Mini manifold, nor is it possible to fit an H4 or HS2 to the automatic-type manifold.

Outside the context of the straight-swap conversion using the carb and manifold assembly from the automatic car, I still personally prefer the H4 SU carburettor to the HS4 unit. Although both have a 1½in bore, the H4 has a choke tube longer by ¾in which encourages better gas flow and hence better performance. On the other hand, the HS4 comes with a quick-lift dashpot assembly as standard.

So far we have only really dealt with Mini tuning using the standard manifolds and a single SU carburettor: with this layout at least 65 to 70bhp is possible. My feeling is that there is not as much to be gained by using twin carburettors or multi-choke carburettors as some people claim, providing the single-carb arrangement is correctly set up and properly tuned. But multi-choke carburettors, or two single-choke units, may improve flexibility and power at lower revs with certain engines. The most usual choices are twin SUs or the DCOE sidedraught Weber (single unit with double choke). Twin Amals are a possibility, but not very popular due to difficulties in tuning and poor fuel economy. I do not intend to cover carburettor design or how to tune them because there are so many variables, and each different combination of engine modifications makes different demands on the carburation. I would advise the purchase of a handbook on whatever type of carburettor one is using, as this will greatly help by explaining tuning and adjustment procedures.

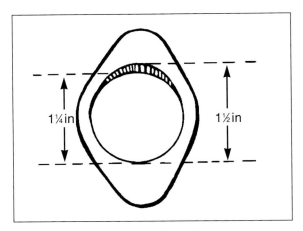

When fitting an H4 SU carburettor to the standard manifold, it is advantageous to enlarge the manifold opening off-centre. This will necessitate relocating the mounting studs.

With the Mini 848cc engine probably the best twin-carburettor arrangement for road use is a pair of 1⅛in H1 SUs, as sold be several leading tuning firms in their off-the-shelf twin-carb conversions. These give not only quite good top-end performance but also excellent flexibility and economy. On the other hand, a DCOE Weber or twin 1¼in H4 SUs are better for racing, especially with a racing camshaft, when poor fuel economy and lack of power at low revs are of no concern.

A number of downdraught carburettors have also been used, including Weber and one or two Japanese makes, but I have no experience of these and therefore cannot comment on their suitability.

Many people, including myself, have used the Reece-Fish carburettor on the 850 Mini. In my opinion this is the ultimate carburettor for the 850, whether for road use, mild competition, rallying or even circuit racing, particularly where regulations prohibit multiple carburettors or twin-choke units. For road use, rallying and occasional speed events, the 1¼in version is best, even if a 731 camshaft is used. But if the engine aspires to diabolical cams, such as the 648/649 or the slightly milder 544, for example in Mini 7 formula racing, then the 1½in Reece-Fish is best. More details on the use of this carburettor can be found in Chapter 13.

Where regulations permit, many people use twin 1½in SUs or a 45 DCOE Weber for competition, but the gains, if any, are frankly only marginal. Certainly, only an engine using the 648 camshaft and a large-valve cylinder head would begin to warrant the use of a Weber or twin SUs

in preference to the Reece-Fish.

Modifying the standard inlet manifold for a different single carburettor is a matter of further experiment along the lines already explained, but it is probably worthwhile buying one from a reputable tuning specialist instead, and may well be cheaper in the long run. Alternatively, for twin carburettors, the standard Cooper and Cooper S manifolds give very satisfactory results at relatively low cost.

It may be necessary under some circumstances to fit a competition Cooper S fuel pump in order to combat fuel surge on right-hand bends. I have never had this trouble on an ordinary Mini but know of others who have, and this has effected a cure. However it is possible that a wrongly set-up carburettor can cause the same problem, and altering the float level on an SU may be all that is required. Fuel surge in the tank can also cause problems when racing, and the only completely effective way to overcome this is to make up a properly baffled tank, ideally one which will sit flat on the boot floor. A nice, round, flat, biscuit-tin-shaped tank will fit neatly in the spare-wheel well.

Larger valves
The further development of the cylinder head involves the fitting of larger inlet valves, the size of which will depend on many factors, not least being the use to which the vehicle is to be put. If the car is intended for competition, it is important to remember that some class regulations prohibit the fitting of larger valves. Remember too that once having fitted larger valves, it is pretty well impossible to go back to the standard size if it turns out to be a mistake. While it can sometimes be done by using seat inserts, these are of questionable reliability, and, if the rest of the head has been properly modified to match, the ports may no longer be suitable for the smaller valves. So unless you are prepared to buy another cylinder head – tread softly!

There is little point in fitting larger exhaust valves in the 850 engine, it is really a waste of time and money. Fitting larger inlet valves involves extensively enlarging the inlet tract: one cannot just fit the valves without also opening out the throats and blending them with the new seats, and the ports will then also need enlarging both to take full advantage of the change and also to avoid a possible counter-productive slowing of gas flow caused by an abrupt transition from standard port to widened throat. As a result of these operations, it is quite possible that low and

The multi-bladed cooling fan can be modified by removing all but four, or even two, pairs of blades, but take care not to upset the balance of the fan. An accurate temperature gauge is a must on a tuned car.

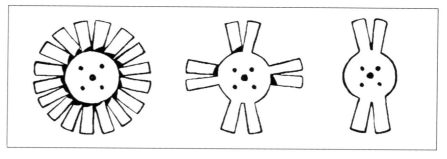

mid-range torque may be ruined, although of course top-end power will usually be improved. In my opinion, the full advantage of this modification can only be gained in conjunction with a more extreme camshaft of the sports or race type, a development which I have included in stage three.

Probably the cheapest and most convenient source of larger inlet valves is the standard Austin/Morris 1100 type, or, to go to the extreme, MG 1100 valves which are even larger. These are of quite good quality and plenty large enough for the 850 engine.

The actual boring out of the valve seats to the requisite size should be undertaken by an expert using accurate engineering equipment, and can usually be done quite cheaply. All further blending, increasing volumes and enlarging ports should be carefully carried out by hand, using rotary files and templates as for any other gas-flowing operation. The valves and seats should be modified in exactly the same way as described for the standard-size components.

Remember that the ultimate size of valve used is governed by the amount by which it is possible to open out the combustion chamber to prevent masking. The earlier warnings should be repeated: one must not risk breaking into waterways, or undercut the gasket. As with so many aspects of tuning, the balance of the different elements is important, and it is better to use a slightly smaller valve than to fit the largest that can be accommodated and cause masking.

Cooling fans
One final worthwhile modification under stage two applies to those Minis equipped with the multi-bladed fan which became standard after 1961. During the first 12 or 18 months production, Minis were fitted with four-bladed

fans. They were made up of two parts each with two blades, bolted to the water pump boss to make a four-bladed unit, but they were very noisy, emitting a high-pitched whine at high revs. To combat this, BMC brought out a one-piece 18-bladed fan: it was much quieter in operation, but not only did it absorb more power, its cooling efficiency was also much less at high revs than that of the original type.

The old four-bladed fans are now scarce and can usually only be obtained from scrapyards. They can be reduced to just two blades by removing one of the portions with obvious benefits in power saving. If the four-bladed type is unavailable, the 18-bladed variety can be reduced by cutting out every other two blades. This should be done very carefully, using a fine hacksaw and finishing off with a hand file, so as not to upset the balance of the fan. For some purposes, it is quite practical to go even further and remove all but four of the blades, leaving just two diametrically opposite pairs, as illustrated.

Note that the original type of four-bladed fan was only homologated for 850 Minis, so that some competition regulations may exclude its use on other models.

Other types of fan, including electric ones, have become available on the accessory after-market over the years, some of which may well be effective. I have little experience of them, and since what little experience I have had does not create a favourable impression of their reliability, I would not use one on a Mini. It is worth remembering that the Mini, with its side-mounted radiator, is very dependent on an effective fan for adequate cooling, especially in hot weather or during competitive motoring, unlike most other cars with front-mounted radiators sitting directly in the blast of moving air. Any fan failure can quickly lead to extreme overheating.

4

850 tuning for competition

Stage three entails much more time and expense because of the extent of the modifications involved and is really only worthwhile when maximum performance is being sought, perhaps for competition, and hence the continual use of very high revs is contemplated. The increase in cost if someone else is to be paid to do the work can be considerable and may deter all but the most prosperous owner. However, with a certain amount of time and effort, the do-it-yourself enthusiast will probably be able to reach this stage for little more financial outlay than might be required for an off-the-shelf stage two conversion.

A worthwhile investment at this stage is a spare cylinder assembly (short engine) unless one is able to take one's vehicle off the road for several weeks at a time. Complete spare engines can if necessary be bought quite cheaply second-hand or from a scrapyard.

The work involves completely stripping the engine down into its component parts and, after modification, very careful and accurate re-assembly with strict adherence to the clearances and tightening torques specified by the manufacturer. Any departure from these can result in an expensive repair bill at a later date.

Camshafts

The first and most important modification is to fit a different camshaft of the sports or race type which gives greater lift and increases the overlap. It is essential when doing this first to have the camshaft housing in the block line-bored to accept bearing liners as used in the Cooper and later engines, if this has not already been done. To ensure correct alignment needs proper workshop equipment so most enthusiasts will find it cheaper and easier to get the job done properly by a specialist: the operation is not a very costly one. The camshaft runs directly in the block without bearing liners in the standard engine and if this is not changed there is every chance that the more highly loaded sport camshaft will seize and wreck the engine.

As has already been outlined, the type of camshaft chosen depends on the use for which the vehicle is intended and on what other tuning modifications are being carried out – the type of manifolds and carburettor/s fitted, the size of the valves, and so on.

It is almost impossible for the average enthusiast to design his own camshaft as this needs considerable expertise and has to be done in conjunction with work on a dynamometer, so it is a matter of taking the advice of a specialist, preferably one with competition experience with a similar car. It is however often possible to use a camshaft originally designed for a different model – the wide range of uses to which the A-series engine has been put is a help here – and once again most specialists are usually forthcoming with answers to sensible enquiries.

A standard Sprite Mk2 or 1071 Cooper S camshaft (BMC part number AEA 630) is an excellent choice for sprint, hill climb or fast road use, giving good torque characteristics at low revs, while the standard 997 or 998cc Cooper camshaft (BMC part number 2A948) gives poor torque low down but very good performance at higher revs. Other useful camshafts are BMC part number C-AEA 731 for road/race use or 544 which is an out-and-out full race cam. Note that this latter camshaft has an extreme specification, in terms of both lift and overlap, and it (or cams reground to a similar profile) may impose excessive strains on the standard valve gear. These strains should be minimized by extensive lightening of the valve gear, enabling the use of the lightest springs that will control valve bounce. The spring retaining collars are quite strong enough, and the oil-shielding collar can be removed.

Somewhere between AEA 630 and 2A948 comes the later standard Cooper S camshaft, number 510, and to any serious tuner this is an obvious first choice for a nicely tuned road car which does occasional competitions, for it retains beautiful flexibility throughout the range.

The exploitation of the 848cc Mini for racing was particularly encouraged by the Mini 7 formula, at first run by the Mini 7 Club and later taken over by the 750 Motor Club under their 'Low Cost Motor Sport' banner. Over the years during which the formula flourished, the cars developed out of all recognition, with more and more extensive modification, later examples regularly producing 85bhp or more. By that stage, almost every standard component had been worked on or replaced by something more suitable from another engine in the A-series range.

For the moment, we will consider problems associated with using the AEA 648 (often called 649) full-race camshaft. This cam is totally unsuitable for road use, and fitting it is not a simple matter. The amount of lift imparted to the valve is, to say the least, extreme: consequently if other components are not suitably changed, it can cause spring crush, in which the coils of the valve spring are closed tight against each other so that no more compression is possible, resulting in a wrecked engine. The camshaft was originally developed for the Cooper S which has longer valves and so allows greater valve travel. In addition, the Cooper S head is fitted with Hidural bronze alloy valve guides to reduce the chance of valve stem seizure.

It is possible to use ordinary valves of the type fitted to the 850/998/1,098cc engines, which are shorter than the S type, but this is far from satisfactory. It necessitates machining the valve spring locating circles in the cylinder head,

sinking the valve seating further into the head, removing metal from the underside of the valve head, and anything else which may allow the valve stem to protrude just a little further when the valve is closed.

But such work can be expensive and one is still left with valves that are inferior in material and design to those of the Cooper S, which are stronger, can be shaped better for ultimate performance and have a top collar and collet arrangement which is far more reliable. The answer is to use Cooper S valves, collars, collets, guides, and preferably also rockers, pedestals, sprockets, timing chain – the lot.

Even then, crush may still occur, though to a lesser degree. Fortunately there is a cheap way out of the problem: fit Ford Cortina 1500 GT valve springs. Since the Ford springs have a slightly smaller inside diameter, this does entail a small amount of machining of the top retaining collar and the bottom inner spring locating collar (competition type) which is a press fit around the top of the valve guide.

A further benefit from the use of these springs is that they give the same performance as the BMC ones in terms of controlling valve bounce but with less actual pressure and hence less strain and wear on the rest of the valve train. This is because, being shorter, they suffer less from harmonic flexing and their own inertia is less. These springs are essential on the Sprite Mk4 head unless even longer valves are used: the spring-locating grooves around the top of the guides cannot be deepened on this head without a very real danger of breaking into the water jacket.

When using the 648/649 camshaft, it is advisable to fit the competition heavy-duty rocker shaft, part number C-AEG-399, which also necessitates replacing one of the ordinary pedestals (No2) with an extra tapped and screwed type like the one already used for No1. The screw in No1 should be cut off flush with the end of the thread so that the oil feed is not impaired.

One of the biggest difficulties with the 850 Mini when using a modified standard cylinder head is to obtain a high enough compression ratio for out-and-out competition purposes. Something like 11:1 is essential when tuning for peak performance with a racing camshaft. Machining the cylinder head face to the very limit will only raise the ratio to about 10:1, more than enough for a fast road engine but not for racing, so one has to resort to additional methods, of which more later.

Ignition timing

As mentioned already, almost all modifications to increase performance necessitate altering the ignition timing and this is especially true when fitting a different camshaft. A new or modified exchange distributor should be obtained, with an advance curve matched to the characteristics of the camshaft. These can be obtained from a reputable tuning shop, or home-brewed as detailed in Chapter 18.

The distributor which I always used was modified from one intended for a Ferguson tractor. The shaft ran in needle roller bearings which made it specially suitable for use at sustained high revs.

Any vacuum advance and retard mechanism fitted to the distributor should be disconnected

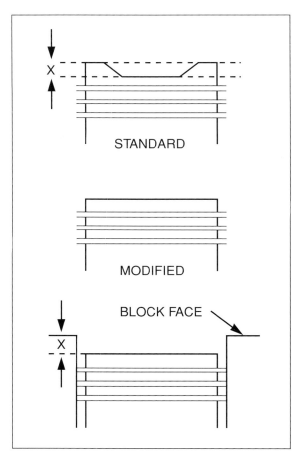

If suitable flat-top pistons are not available, it is possible to modify the standard pistons by machining the crowns flat, but an equivalent amount will then have to be machined from the top face of the cylinder block.

and the manifold tube sealed. If left connected, it may cause over-advanced ignition at high revs and that can quickly lead to a wrecked engine.

It is difficult to be specific about the timing to use on the 850 Mini because of the variety of camshafts and other modifications that may be employed, but it will probably be somewhere between TDC and 7 degrees advance for static setting. Trial and error is the only way of finding the optimum.

Pistons

The standard pistons have a concave crown and should be replaced by flat-top solid-skirt pistons. If these are unobtainable, the crowns of the standard pistons should be machined flat and the face of the block machined by a corresponding amount, the net result being flat-top pistons giving a much increased compression ratio – in the region of 11:1 depending on the work that has been carried out on the head. Modifying the pistons in this way is quite safe on the 850 engine, and even though the pistons are not of the solid-skirt variety they are quite suitable and reliable. On engines with a much-increased bore, however, I would not recommend such action because the increased strain put on the piston crowns can cause breakage. While it is practical to modify the pistons oneself, providing care is taken, the block has to be precision machined so I would always have the pistons machined at the same time.

Having done this, the next step is to shape the valve pockets into the top of the block and pistons as necessary when using a higher-lift camshaft. The depth and width of the pockets depends on the camshaft and valves being used and on the amount which has been machined off the cylinder head.

If one inspects certain standard pistons in the BMC A-series range, it will be seen that some have slots through the piston body in the ring groove under the bottom oil-control ring (I have found one example of this type to be used in the MG 1100 engine). With such pistons, the compression ratio should be limited to about 10:1. At higher compression ratios these slots tend to be forced shut – in other words they weaken the piston and allow it to distort – with obvious disastrous consequences to the piston and possibly the rest of the engine as well. Many pistons have slots beneath the bottom ring in the piston skirt and, though these are not exactly desirable because theoretically they also weaken the piston (drilled holes are better), they usually prove safe in practice, even on full-race engines: I have never known this type of slot to cause trouble.

A weakness with this engine is in the clamp bolts which secure the gudgeon pins to the connecting rods. These bolts have been known to break, a tendency which is more pronounced on 997cc Cooper and enlarged-capacity 850-based engines. Some competition regulations forbid their replacement, but where possible the connecting rods should be replaced by the type which incorporate fully floating little ends. I personally have never had this trouble with the standard rod in the 850 engine, but I know of one or two disastrous failures. It may be possible to obtain specially made rods but these are invariably very expensive. A convenient source of cheap and excellent connecting rods is the standard 998cc Mini/Elf/Cooper engine or the 1,098cc Austin/Morris 1100 engine. Do not use the very earliest type of Morris 1100 connecting rods, as these had very weak little ends.

These rods are fully floating with the gudgeon pin retained by circlips. This means that when using standard 850 pistons it will be necessary to get circlip grooves machined in the pistons. Additionally, the 850 piston gudgeon bosses have to be filed or machined to increase the distance between them, as these rods have wider little ends than the 850 pattern. This is quite a simple operation providing care is taken, and a fine hand file is an adequate tool.

It is advisable to use round wire circlips of the heaviest gauge possible, obtainable from piston suppliers. The circlip grooves should be machined about ⅛in in from the surface of the piston and, needless to say, should have a rounded profile to accept the round wire circlip. The circlips are supplied with one end of the wire bent over forming a tag to facilitate their removal from the piston. But these tags must be cut off, and the ends of the wire given a nice radius on a grindstone. Otherwise they can break off in the engine, or allow the gudgeon pin to push the circlip out: in both cases the results can be disastrous.

Having cut off the tags, it is almost impossible to remove the circlips, and hence the gudgeon pins, unless further piston modifications are carried out. This is, however, fairly simple. My method is to use a very small high-speed drill, about ¹⁄₁₆in diameter, and drill in from the outside of the piston to the bottom of the circlip groove, finishing off with a very fine needle file. This leaves a small opening, nicely radiused to reduce the chance of causing breakage, running into the base of the circlip groove, through which a small

screwdriver can be inserted to flick the circlip out. Methods involving the use of hacksaw blades or small files are less satisfactory because they tend to leave an untidy slot and cause unnecessary piston bruising. A slot which is rough or not rounded can easily form the starting point for a crack in the highly stressed piston.

The gudgeon pins should have their ends tapered off at approximately 45 degrees for about ³⁄₁₆in so that they just protrude through the circlip. This prevents the gudgeon pin forcing the circlip out of its groove, as can so easily happen. If the pin is tapered, end thrust will tend to force the circlip back into the groove.

I have dealt with this modification at some length because it has long been the traditional method of dispensing with the pinch-bolt form of gudgeon-pin retention and will probably remain so. It usually proved reliable when Minis were not revved much above 7,000rpm. Later, though, new techniques, new materials and new components combined to push the rev limit on racing 850s to well over 8,000rpm, bringing new problems and rendering circlip little ends completely unsuitable. At very high revs, the circlips close up because of the forces exerted on them (the heavier the clip the greater the forces) and drop out of the piston.

If that doesn't happen, crankshaft whip causes the connecting rods to run at an angle and then, no matter how freely the rod normally runs on the gudgeon pin – I used to make my pins so loose that at human body heat they would fall out of the rod under their own weight – it will seize on the pin and drive it with considerable force against the circlip. If the ends of the pin are tapered it can sometimes even push the side out of the piston against the cylinder wall. Most unpleasant!

All these problems are overcome by changing over to the set-up used on the Cooper S, with an interference fit between gudgeon pin and connecting rod. This is really the simplest method of all and certainly the most reliable. The bronzed bushes in the little end of the 998/1100 connecting rod must be removed and replaced by steel bushes. Care must be taken to ensure that the bore in the new bush runs exactly parallel with the big end bore. Standard 998/1100 gudgeon pins can be used, pressed into the little end with an interference fit of between 0.0015 and 0.0025in (1½ to 2½ thou). The gudgeon pin should be a finger-tight press fit in the piston. The 850 pistons need no modification for this method of fitting other than increasing the

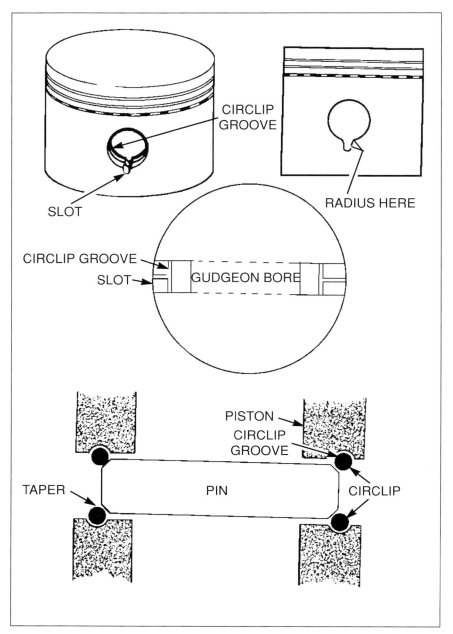

CIRCLIP GROOVE

SLOT

RADIUS HERE

CIRCLIP GROOVE

SLOT

GUDGEON BORE

PISTON

CIRCLIP GROOVE

TAPER

PIN

CIRCLIP

The standard pistons can be modified to take fully floating gudgeon pins retained by circlips. A slot leading into the circlip groove is necessary to allow the circlips to be removed. Tapering the ends of the gudgeon pins is recommended: end thrust will then tend to push the circlips into the grooves rather than forcing them out.

distance between the gudgeon bosses inside.

While this technique is simple in concept, it has the drawback that special tools and jigs are required for assembly and separation, and the services of a specialist engineer should be sought.

One word of warning. Some people heat the little end of the rod to facilitate fitting the gudgeon pin: my advice is, at all costs don't – it can cause eventual breakage.

Clutch and flywheel

The extra power obtained from a highly tuned engine can cause clutch problems such as rapid wear and slip, and therefore necessitates strengthening the clutch springs. For Minis with a coil-spring clutch, the first step is to fit standard Cooper outer springs along with special inner springs, thus giving double clutch springs. Secondly. it is advisable to use a competition driven plate which has the friction lining both bonded and riveted on, making it less prone to break up under heavy loads and at high revs. Such a clutch will have a very heavy pedal and will tend to be unprogressive, either in or out, with little tendency to slip.

For cars with a diaphragm-spring clutch, strengthening is still necessary, achieved in this case by replacing the spring with a stronger one obtained either from a tuning shop or as standard equipment for a more powerful model. An extra strong competition diaphragm is unnecessary on any 850 Mini and would merely impose extra stresses and strains. I have always found the standard 1275 Cooper S diaphragm, colour-coded blue, perfectly adequate on my 850 racer, and it is a satisfactory road clutch too.

As a result of several nasty episodes where over-lightened standard flywheels have disintegrated at high revs, the Special Tuning department marketed a lightweight replacement in forged steel, but it seemed very expensive to me and proved for some reason to have a nasty habit of welding itself to the crankshaft. Frankly, I use a judiciously lightened standard flywheel, but the decision is yours – 'You pays yer money and takes yer choice!'

The lightening operation on a standard flywheel should be limited to removing not more than ½in of metal from the non-friction face (the diaphragm side) and possibly machining small grooves in the sides of the starter ring, together with radiusing off all sharp edges near the periphery. Do not forget to make spacers onto which the diaphragm can be fitted to compensate for the thickness of metal removed from the flywheel. The three-lugged pressure plate can also be lightened by machining it to a triangular shape or removing metal from between the lugs, but do not reduce its thickness. Balancing of the entire assembly, including the crankshaft, is essential after lightening and, as already indicated, this is a job for the properly equipped specialist.

On re-assembly, location of the clutch and flywheel depends on the crankshaft taper and consequently all surfaces, both on crank and flywheel, should be rendered completely free of oil film by cleaning with a suitable solvent which evaporates without residue (taking due precautions over adequate ventilation and removing any fire risk). Using petrol, paraffin or the like tends to leave a film which can cause the flywheel to spin on the crankshaft at high revs, with obviously drastic results.

Prior to this, the flywheel should be carefully lapped onto the crankshaft taper using fine lapping compound, Brasso and Brasso diluted with paraffin. Ignore the manufacturer's torque setting of 115lb/ft for the flywheel retaining bolt and use 140lb/ft – on my racer, I use 200lb/ft.

Crankshafts

Up to about December, 1963, the crankshafts on 848cc Minis were very weak and continual use of revs in excess of 6,500 inevitably caused failures, even on carefully assembled and fully balanced engines, though the danger could be reduced by fitting a Cooper vibration damper. After that date, the crankshafts were considerably strengthened and the later pattern is safe at 7,000 to 7,500rpm: occasional use of 8,000rpm is quite common, especially if a vibration damper is fitted.

A special hardened competition crankshaft marketed by the BMC Special Tuning department carries part number C-AEG 515. I always use this crank and take it up to 8,500rpm. It is necessary on such an engine to use the large-diameter vibration damper, the second standard type on the Cooper S, which bolts onto the crankshaft pulley. The one-piece dampers, 1100 or early S type, are not much good, largely because their smaller diameter prevents them doing the job for which they were intended at anything above about 7,000rpm.

Do not use the standard early type pressed-steel crankshaft pulley when using a damper: use the later Cooper S solid machined steel type. The crankshaft pulley bolt should be fitted with the competition locking washer or preferably using a locking compound, and, after finally tightening it to about 150lb/ft, lock-wire it in place using thin welding rod and not copper wire, which is too soft.

One problem common to nearly all Mini-type racing engines is the rapid disintegration of the phosphor-bronze bushes in the primary gear, particularly if the extra-strong orange-coded competition diaphragm-spring clutch is used. The answer from the Special Tuning department at Abingdon was a steel-backed bush in a primary gear, complete with a special washer. The bushes are not available on their own, one must buy a complete primary gear assembly.

The standard big-end bearing shells are quite adequate but the main-bearing shells should be replaced by a heavy-duty steel-backed type. All main-bearing housing bolts should be replaced and the centre bearing cap checked for cracking. Providing regulations allow it, the centre cap

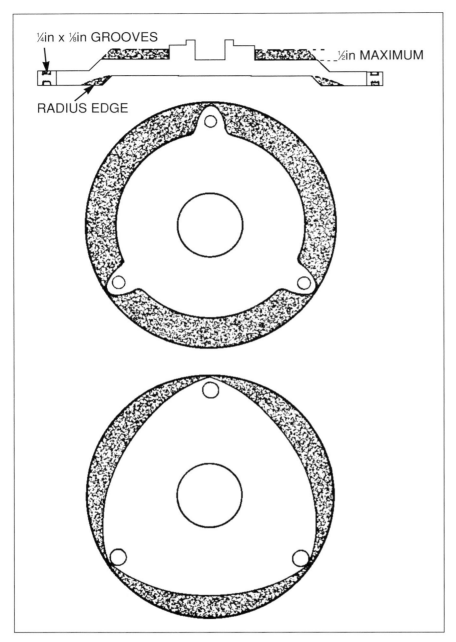

¼in x ⅛in GROOVES

½in MAXIMUM

RADIUS EDGE

Section of flywheel (top) showing where metal can be removed: excessive lightening can be dangerous. The pressure plate can be lightened by modifying it to either of the shapes shown below, but remember that it must subsequently be balanced.

should be reinforced with a good quality steel strap. On my 850 racer I use a complete new steel centre main-bearing cap, line-bored to match the block.

Oil pump

Later Minis have a Cooper-type oil pump as standard. Early cars should have the original-equipment pump replaced by one of the later type which is less prone to wear and has a better output. The oil pressure obtained will ultimately depend on the strength of the pressure-relief valve spring, always assuming, of course, that the rest of the engine is in perfect condition and the oil filter is not clogged. I have always found that the standard spring gives perfectly adequate pressure: excessive pressure can cause the failure of oil seals.

Competition Minis often suffer from oil surge in the sump, and to overcome this most tuning

40

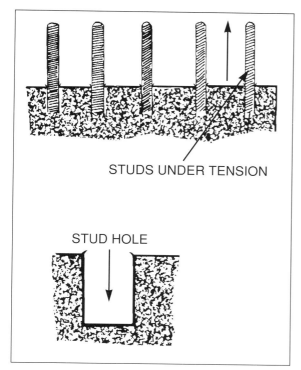

STUDS UNDER TENSION

STUD HOLE

All openings in the block faces should be inspected for roughness which may impair sealing. Removing studs and lightly countersinking the threaded holes during overhaul is recommended.

specialists sell modified pick-up pipes (Special Tuning's version is part number C-AHT 54) which draw oil from the centre of the sump, not from one side as standard, thereby reducing the danger that surge will allow the lubrication system momentarily to run dry.

The oil pump can be modified by 'gas flowing' its ports to give improved flow and better pressure. This merely involves radiusing and thinning the lips of the ports so as to increase port area without increasing its dimension on the outer pump face.

Some later, larger-engined cars have a modified oil-pump drive, a change which affects interchangeability of both pumps and camshafts: more details in Chapter 17.

Exhaust system
A good extractor exhaust manifold is useful when using a vigorous race camshaft, and probably the cheapest are the MG 1100 or standard Cooper manifolds. These are just as effective and much cheaper than many of the better-looking specialist

manifolds. The MG version has the advantage that it can be used in conjunction with a standard exhaust pipe, whereas the Cooper type necessitates enlarging the pipe diameter right through and in some cases this can actually decrease the power over the workable rev range. However, it is fairly safe to say that this will not apply to a fully modded twin-carb racing Mini.

Remember that at this level of tuning the combinations of pipe length and diameter, camshaft overlap and lift, ignition settings and carburation are almost infinitely variable, each set-up giving a slightly different result. A good example of this was provided by my own experience with exhaust pipe design. Two layouts were both used with the same engine, camshaft, carburettor, manifolds and so on, a simple swap from one to the other being the only change. One set-up, with a full-length standard-diameter pipe, emerging at the back of the vehicle, with no silencer but with the last 18in of pipe increased in diameter by $\frac{5}{16}$in, needed an E3 needle in the carb and gave very good low to middle-range performance but little power above 6,000rpm.

The other set-up involved cutting the standard-diameter pipe just aft of the front bulkhead and fitting to this a pipe larger in diameter by ¼in, bent so that it came out under the passenger's door. A standard Austin A40 silencer box, with nothing inside it, was welded in 14in from the end of this second pipe, giving the effect of an expansion box and forming a sort of reverse-cone megaphone. An M needle (much weaker than the E3) was used in the HS2 SU carburettor, and this combination gave no power below 4,500rpm but was still giving excellent power at the 7,000rpm rev limit. Thus I could simply and quickly alter the car's characteristics according to circumstances. Both systems cost me about £1 for the two!

Other engine modifications
The cylinder head studs have a tendency to pull up through the block and raise a rough fraze on the block face. This may cause the head gasket to make a poor seal and consequently it is advisable during overhaul to remove the studs and lightly countersink the threaded holes to remove this roughness. The stud holes in the head should be similarly countersunk.

Under extremely hard driving conditions such as those encountered in competition, the engine oil can get excessively hot and cease to provide adequate lubrication, causing bearing failure or even worse maladies. This should be rectified by fitting an oil cooler. Care should be taken to ensure that all the pipes and connections are sound and suitable for the pressures under which they will be working, especially when hot. Do not be tempted to buy cheap gimmicky fittings, they are not much good and in the end a waste of money. The bigger the cooling area the better, and always use a radiator with proper gills.

With a change in carburation, you have reached the stage where it may be worthwhile fitting a different cylinder head with a better basic design and larger valves as standard, such heads being found on the Cooper, Mk2 and Mk3 Sprite and MG 1100. These, when fully modified as described later, may give better results than the somewhat crude fully modified 850 head. But it is important to bear in mind the difference in capacity, and hence in gas volumes, between the basic Mini engine and these other versions: if, for example, using a Sprite Mk4 head on an 850cc engine, as I did successfully in my Mini racer, do not increase the port size as to do so would slow rather than accelerate gas flow and destroy low and mid-range torque.

The 850 Mini can be bored out to about 960cc, but I cannot see the point of such an operation when you can usually buy a more reliable standard 998cc unit just as cheaply. The tuning procedure for the bored-out engine would be almost identical to that adopted for the 998cc version so there is absolutely nothing to be gained.

I would suggest that even for road use a heavy-duty oil is a good idea. If serious competition is contemplated, use a castor-based oil (replaced more recently by special high-specification synthetic competition oils), as these retain much better viscosity at high temperatures. Always warm the engine up gently (the same applies to a lesser extent with ordinary heavy-duty oils) and until normal working temperatures are reached do not exceed 2,000rpm otherwise you may well 'run the bearings'.

Do not use the standard sparking plugs on a tuned engine. They run too hot and, besides wearing out very rapidly, can cause holes in pistons, especially if the mixture is a bit weak. I would recommend Champion N3 or N9Y on all but the most highly tuned engines which are being used for racing, when N63R or N62Y may be found more suitable. Other manufacturers, of course, make comparable plugs, but I have no experience of any other than Champion. More on ignition can be found in Chapter 18.

A rev counter and good oil pressure and water temperature gauges are invaluable in tuning and competition driving. Remember however that electric water temperature gauges are very inaccurate: use the bulb and capillary type if at all possible, even if it means replacing an existing electric one.

5

Tuning for economy

It is often assumed that tuning an engine for speed will have an adverse effect on fuel consumption. This is not necessarily true of a conversion intended for road use. In fact, I would go so far as to say that if a normal road conversion causes an increase in fuel consumption, there is something wrong with the conversion. There are, of course, exceptions to this rule – a lot depends on the state of tune of the engine as manufactured and on its precise characteristics. But I have always noticed an improvement in fuel consumption when modifying an engine, certainly with the Mini power unit. A Mini Traveller I owned did 35mpg when driven hard in standard form: modified, average consumption was 42mpg. Gentle driving did not produce any improvement worth considering, only about 2mpg.

There are other popular misconceptions. Probably the most common is the idea that fitting a larger but otherwise similar carburettor, or changing to twin carburettors, reduces economy. This again is generally speaking untrue, unless the change involves adopting a basically uneconomical type of carburettor, replacing an SU with Amals for example. But this assumes, of course, that the carburation is properly set up and adjusted, and that the carburettor is neither too large nor too small for the engine in question. When I first fitted the 1½in carb I was down to 25mpg, but two days' feverish sorting gave me 42mpg with no reduction in performance. It is this question of fuel consumption which often distinguishes the really good tuning firm from the bodgers and graunchers.

There is of course a broad equation between fuel consumed and power produced, and enormous increases in power are not obtained without using more fuel. But within narrower limits, consumption is determined by the efficiency with which the engine converts fuel into mechanical energy. The point is that when you tune an engine for extra performance, what you do in general terms is to improve its efficiency. You increase the efficiency with which fuel mixture enters the cylinders, improve the efficiency with which it is burned, leaving less unburnt residue, and improve the efficiency with which exhaust gases are removed. All things being equal, this must give better fuel economy.

Racing engines are a special and somewhat misleading case. Their development is based on the assumption that economy is of no consequence. Without going into great detail, race-tuned engines often use more fuel than they actually burn. A major factor here is camshaft design and the desire to have the cylinder filled only with fuel mixture at the point of ignition. The cooling effect of fuel-rich mixture on valves and pistons is sometimes a consideration too.

To return to more normal and practical tuning for road use, how would I tune for economy and how would this compare with my tuning for speed? The first thing to say is that there would be no basic differences. An efficiently gas-flowed cylinder head with raised compression is essential. Inlet and exhaust manifolds must be gas-flowed

The external woodwork applied to some Mini estates is purely cosmetic, not structural, as evidenced by this common-sense all-steel version, a highly versatile little car. This one is a Morris Mini Traveller.

or replaced by special free-flow components. If gas-flowing dictated fitting larger valves and this then necessitated fitting a larger carburettor, I would fit one. If, on the other hand, worthwhile gas-flowing of the cylinder head is possible without increasing valve size or carburettor size, that is a good route to follow for economy.

The requirements of road motoring rule out a wild camshaft anyway. That aside, the only difference between speed and economy tuning is likely to be in the actual carburettor settings. Tuning for high performance demands a slightly rich mixture setting, whereas tuning for economy demands a mixture just a little on the weak side. Needless to say, all the other operations aimed at keeping an engine working with the greatest efficiency, such as correct plugs, points and tappet settings, reducing internal friction where possible, and so on, are common to both aims in tuning.

No major differences in procedure, then, and I most certainly would not try to weaken the mixture beyond what is broadly the correct setting purely for economy, because over-weak mixture brings with it the danger of burnt exhaust valves and, in extremis, melted pistons. Overall gearing can have some bearing on economy, and raising the final-drive ratio (see Chapter 6) can be beneficial if the car is under-geared to start with: but over-do it and you will be worse off, not better, because you will have to spend more time in the intermediate gears to get the engine to pull.

To put all the theory into some kind of practical perspective, I am going to relate the case-history of my own everyday road transport over a period of about 18 months, which should

be fairly typical of any converted road car. The vehicle in question was a 1966 Austin Mini-Traveller, the kind with all-steel bodywork. In 18 months it covered something like 40,000 miles – the precise figure was lost because the mileometer packed up. I took delivery of the Traveller in completely standard form save for Jaguar 3.8 Mk2 headlamps with 70-watt main beams, a most worthwhile alteration.

The car was run-in for 4,000 miles and then an old, spare head was fitted so that work could begin on the new 850 head. It was fully treated as described earlier in the book. It was machined to take 0.100in off the face, and Morris 1100 inlet valves (not the larger MG 1100 type) were fitted. Standard exhaust valves were retained. Single, extra-strong valve springs were used, though I did not fit steel shims under the collets. The combustion chambers were carefully balanced and the standard valve guides were reshaped. The manifolds were gas-flowed and matched to the head. Initially, to keep costs down, I stuck to the original 1¼in HS2 SU carburettor.

When it was running again, I found that, although performance was much better, it still seemed strangled. The 0-60mph time was approximately 19 seconds. I set to work on the carburettor, fitting a quick-lift dashpot assembly and E3 needle. This reduced the 0-60mph time to 17 seconds, still not good enough, even though a Traveller is 1cwt heavier than the ordinary saloon. I fitted a number 6 needle: acceleration time dropped to 15 seconds for 0-60mph and the top speed was 85 to 90mph (fifth-wheel reading of 88mph on a short straight) but fuel consumption was a disastrous 26mpg, bad enough to break the bank! It was obviously running far too rich, even to the point of cutting out at the top end.

Well, I tried radiusing the carburettor piston and rounding off the carburettor intake, but all to no avail. Finally I admitted defeat and fitted a second-hand 1½in H4 SU on a suitably modified inlet manifold. A quick-lift dashpot and RLB needle were fitted, and it was absolutely fabulous. With only cylinder head, manifold and carburettor modifications, I could see off any ordinary Cooper and quite a few Cooper S types, including my mate's standard 1275 Hydrolastic S. We recorded 0-60mph in 12 seconds: we have often been accused of over-optimism with that figure, but it was checked and double-checked on several watches. Top speed on the flat was over 90mph and under ideal conditions an indicated 105mph could be obtained. The governing factor was valve-bounce in top! And petrol consumption was a very acceptable 42mpg.

Lightened pushrods and rockers were the only other engine mods, and the car was otherwise standard apart from Michelin X tyres. The brakes and suspension were standard, and although the former were more than adequate, I am afraid that the same cannot be said for the latter. It was horrible – talk about rock and roll! The net result was three destroyed drive-shaft joints within three months. I was accused of brutal driving by my garage (partially true!) to which my reply was, as always, a few choice oaths directed at the standard shock absorbers as fitted to Minis.

A pair of Konis was fitted to the front only, adjusted to soft settings. Not only did this transform the former 'ship-at-sea' ride but it also cured the drive-shaft unreliability, no doubt by preventing excessive front suspension travel. The Konis were fitted at 11,000 miles: on selling the car at something over 40,000 miles, no further drive-shafts had been needed. Decent front shock absorbers might well have saved BLMC their cost and more in warranty claims for rubber universal joints, I reckon!

At the same time as I fitted the shock absorbers, I fitted an SPQR engine stabilizer kit, consisting of small cones and rods under the gearbox. That reduced the tendency to snatch and judder and further improved the handling by cutting out a lot of engine and transmission rock which is otherwise transferred to the front wheels. The front brakes were relined with Ferodo AM4 at 25,000 miles and were only half worn when the car was sold. Other than the usual Mini mods of an SPQR throttle cable, steering column adjuster and straight-through Sprite Mk1 silencer, no other deviations from standard were made.

Really and truly, this was a fabulous little bomb. The performance was quite surprising, to judge by people's faces when they were passed, being at least equal to a Cortina GT. The fuel economy was great, and after 40,000 miles it was still doing 400 miles to a pint of Duckhams Q20/50 oil.

In the last three months of my ownership of the Traveller I used it for towing my Mini 7 racer and this it did very well in the dry, being capable of 70mph and 35mpg with the trailer behind. Some 3,000 miles were covered like that. But there were two big snags when towing. You could not stop under any circumstances, and any road, even a straight, was lethal if it rained. After spinning the whole lot twice at 15mph, I decided to trade the old faithful in for a new (whisper!) 1500 Cortina Super. (Since those days, changes in the regulations pertaining to the relative weights of towing vehicles and trailers have effectively outlawed towing a Mini behind a Mini and similar acts of applied optimism – perhaps it's just as well!)

The only expenses other than petrol, oil and those drive-shafts had been five new Michelin Xs (two more needed at the time of sale) new wheel-cylinder rubbers, one new exhaust system, two fan belts, eight sets of Champion N9Y plugs, three sets of points and a new clutch thrust bearing which I never did fit – it had been noisy for several months and finally went kaput the day I parted with the car. All in all, one of the most reliable and faithful cars I have ever had or am likely to have.

6

Transmission

It is not the purpose of these pages to explain how to strip and rebuild a Mini gearbox, nor indeed to cover any other routine mechanical work, details of which are comprehensively described and illustrated in the factory Workshop Manual which is a must for any ambitious do-it-yourself enthusiast. What is intended is to explain what gears can be used and with what effect.

The type of gear ratios you can use may depend on the gearbox you happen to have, as there have been a number of changes over the years. Plain-bearing gear clusters were fitted at first but, after the mid-1960s, ordinary Mini gearboxes were basically similar inside to the contemporary Cooper S type, having needle-roller bearings fitted. But most good tuning experts can modify the older gearbox to accept the later parts: I would not advise any but the best equipped and most proficient enthusiast to attempt the modifications himself, and buying another second-hand box may or may not be a cheaper alternative. The all-synchromesh gearbox, which was phased in progressively after the advent of the Mk2 bodyshell with its larger rear window, is significantly different from all the earlier, non-synchro-first boxes.

Dealing first with the earlier gearbox in its unmodified form, there is just one alternative. You can fit standard 997cc Cooper gears, which, while not strictly close ratio, are somewhat closer than those of the ordinary Mini and, used in conjunction with a 3.9:1 or 4.1:1 final drive, can provide some improvement. I would not,

however, regard the benefits as sufficient to warrant any great expense, but it could be a useful modification if the parts happened to be to hand. The ideal very close ratio gears for this box, with competition in mind, were available through specialists such as Speedwell, but limited production made them much more expensive than any standard BMC set.

If the box has been modified or is of the later needle-roller, three-synchro type, there is a much wider choice. Standard Cooper 998cc or Cooper S gears offer slightly closer ratios than the ordinary Mini type but, as with the earlier Cooper set already mentioned, the benefits are not enormous. More significant are the optional alternative gears specified by BMC for the Cooper S which offer the ultimate in close ratios at relatively moderate cost. They can be obtained in either helical-cut or straight-cut form. (More about straight-cut gears in our coverage of the Cooper S in Chapter 11).

These gears can be fitted to almost any of the transverse A-series boxes, though in the case of non-Cooper S or pre-1966 units it will be necessary to carry out certain machining operations and to purchase several extra parts to replace existing components. Just what has to be done will depend upon the exact vintage of the box in question, those prior to 1963 needing more work than later examples. A study of the official parts book will show what is needed.

While on the subject of gearboxes and their interchangeability, it should be pointed out that, although there is generally little difference between various boxes of the same vintage, there was until around September 1967 one big difference between those fitted to the Cooper S and all the other transverse units. This affected the casing rather than the internals of the box. To cope with the longer stroke, thicker crankshaft and different main-bearing journal alignment of the S engine, the gearbox casing was made wider than that of other models. People who tried to fit S engines to ordinary Mini boxes soon discovered that the crankshaft fouled the sides of the casing. If it was a 970 or 1,071cc unit that you were trying to fit, then in most cases all that was necessary was to grind a little metal from the inside of the casing. But for a 1,275cc engine, the amount of metal needing to be removed was excessive and a new gearbox was really the only answer. One or two people tried widening the casing by cutting it and then argon-arc welding it together again, but it was a very tricky operation and there were big problems with distortion. Fortunately it was not long before the manufacturers started to make all gearboxes alike in respect of major dimensions.

People sometimes ask about fitting the Mini Cooper remote gearchange to an ordinary Mini. This can be done (although in my opinion it is unnecessary) but it is not quite the simple task it is often imagined to be. It involves removing the gearbox and fitting a new casting to the back of the final-drive housing. The casting forms part of the housing when they are bolted together and strictly speaking the two should be line-bored together to ensure accurate matching, although in practice many enthusiasts have found that it worked all right without.

The all-synchromesh gearbox may look just like any earlier Mini box externally but internally it is very different, and must be regarded as a complete departure from the older type. The only practical interchangeability between the two lies in the differential and its housing and even there swapping parts involves, theoretically at least, line-boring as already mentioned. The original Cooper S close-ratio gears will not fit an all-synchro box and it is not a practical proposition to modify the box to make them fit, neither can any other gears or major components from the earlier design be introduced into an all-synchro casing. In due course, though, Special Tuning introduced close-ratio gears to suit the new box. Care needs to taken, therefore, when buying parts either new or second-hand, to check their suitability.

After the production of the Mk2 Mini and then the Clubman really got under way, the newer remote-control type of gearbox casing became standard. Even those Minis without remote changes, basic models and vans, had the same casing: in place of the remote change mechanism was an adaptor allowing the long 'magic wand' lever to be fitted. To convert to remote in this case simply involves removing the adaptor, cutting another hole in the floor and bolting the remote mechanism into place.

This extra degree of interchangeability, however, did not extend to the internal components, the all-synchro boxes remaining a distinct type and the three-synchro boxes staying like the earlier units inside. It is true, though, that an all-synchro box will mate up to any A-series transverse engine. That could be useful if you are using second-hand assemblies, but frankly I have never considered this swap really worthwhile just for the sake of it, particularly if competition is intended. The extra synchromesh is an extra complication, just something else to go wrong, and in my opinion no self-respecting racer or rally driver would rely on synchromesh to help change gear anyway.

Some people still think that the 1100 and Mini remote gearchanges are similar and interchangeable. There is, however, a major difference. The Cooper, Cooper S and Mini Mk2 remotes attach direct to the rear of the differential housing with four bolts. The 1100 set-up has a thick rubber block which fits between the forward end of the remote tunnel and the back of the diff housing. In addition, the two components fit together at a different angle to those on the Mini. Unfortunately, the rubber block introduces a considerable loss of precision to the change, making it less than ideal, particularly for competition. I well remember a friend of mine who raced a Mini 7 formula car complaining that he could not select gear properly since fitting an 1100 gearbox, these usually being cheaper on the second-hand market than the Cooper type. I suggested that he might replace the standard rubber with a steel or light alloy block, thus making the joint rigid. This worked perfectly and completely cured the selection problems. Since then I have tried it on several other cars equally successfully.

When racing a Mini, one problem which is often encountered in the heat of the moment is difficulty in selecting third gear because the lever tends to go right across into the reverse gate. The only sure remedy is to fit some kind of lock to blank out the reverse gear. Some people have used a cable-operated linkage but I think that is

Rallycross, here at Lydden Hill, is one of the forms of motorsport in which the Mini has had a very long and successful career. The Perspex windscreen with cutouts is one of many ploys tried to maintain some visibility through the barrage of flying mud.

unnecessarily complicated. The simplest answer is to make up a steel plate about 2in wide and bolt it rigidly, either to the floor or to the gearlever housing, in such a position that the lever is prevented from passing beyond the third/fourth plane. This may sound crude but, providing care is taken to make the plate sufficiently strong (I use ⅜in steel) and position it accurately, it is very effective. It is possible to make the plate in two sections, one of which is hinged and can be lifted to allow the selection of reverse gear. The basic idea can be adapted to suit your preferences and available materials.

So much for what can be done to the various gearboxes. The question remains, what is the purpose of fitting closer-ratio gears? The size of the difference between adjacent gear ratios determines the size of the change in engine revs when you change up or down at a given road speed. Standard production engines work effectively over a relatively large rev range, commonly something like 5,000rpm. An engine tuned for racing may well have a much smaller

usable range, say 1,500rpm, the reduction being part of the price paid for a higher power output. So on a standard car, large differences between gear ratios are tolerable because a drop of perhaps 3,000rpm still leaves the engine able to pull cleanly. And widely-spaced ratios suit the average motorist who likes to pull away from rest at 800rpm and yet reach 80mph on the motorway, the former demanding a very low first gear and the latter a relatively high top gear. But this is no good for our racer. A drop of more than 1,500rpm takes it right 'off the cam' and leaves it spluttering and in danger of stalling.

Since gearbox design dictates that top gear nearly always has to remain constant – gearbox ratio, not final-drive ratio – we must resort to altering the ratios below. So we make the new first gear a bit lower than the standard second and cram the new second and third into the ratio range previously occupied by one gear, thus reducing the gap in ratio between adjacent gears and reducing the drop in revs when changing up to, say, 1,000rpm. Simple, isn't it?

With a big engine and bags of torque, the answer may well be yes: with a small engine, no. First gear is now too high to allow the vehicle to make a reasonably quick and easy get-away from rest. One answer is to put in a fifth, lower ratio, which is possible but very, very expensive unless mass-produced. The other answer is to lower the final-drive ratio and hence the overall gearing but then, of course the maximum speed in top gear, dictated by the engine's rev limit, is reduced and a fifth gear, an overdrive top, is needed again.

But cost dictates that many small-engined racers such as 850 Minis use four-speed boxes in spite of a narrow rev range. The practical answer, as so often, is a degree of compromise: one simply has to tolerate a lot of clutch slip on departing from rest and work at making the engine reliable at high revs to provide a high enough top speed.

It should be clear, of course, that fitting ultra-close ratios to a standard engine will simply result in a car that is unpleasant to drive, either overgeared in bottom and hence difficult to pull away in, or undergeared in top and consequently fussy, slow and uneconomical.

Final-drive ratios

The overall gearing is determined by the final drive and, in practical terms, selecting a different ratio is often the simplest and most cost-effective way of modifying the transmission to suit a tuned engine or to adapt the car to a specific form of competition. Remember that a higher final-drive ratio raises the overall gearing, and higher ratios are numerically lower. For example, a car with a 3.9:1 final drive is higher geared than one with a 4.1:1 final drive.

Selection, again, is a matter of compromise, weighing the use to which the car is to be put against the characteristics of the engine and so on. Generally speaking, standard cars have just about the right ratio. Lower overall gearing will improve low and middle-range acceleration but may limit top speed and will certainly make the car less pleasant for long-distance cruising. It's all a matter of 'horses for courses'. For example, many racing Minis, competing mostly on short and twisty circuits, have top speeds of only 105 to 110mph and need to rev to 8,000rpm even then: their acceleration, however, is fantastic.

Higher overall gearing will not, of course, increase the overall performance of the car without an increase in power from the engine. But if the engine is tuned, a higher ratio may suit conditions like, for example, continuous high-speed driving in top gear, reducing revs for a given speed and so reducing noise and possibly fuel consumption too. The penalty is some loss of acceleration. Personally, for road use I would keep the standard final-drive ratio unless at least 60% of my motoring was on motorways, even if I had a tuned engine.

The choice of ratios for the Mini is quite wide. Interchangeability of final drives between the various transverse A-series units is complete (with the exception of some limited-slip differentials). What fits the first Minis ever made will also fit the latest 1300 or the Cooper S, and vice versa, the only qualification being that the crown wheel and pinion are a matched pair so both must be changed together.

In the case of a tuned 850, the standard final-drive ratio of 3.75:1 can with advantage be changed to 3.9:1 or 4.1:1 to give lower gearing. This may not be such a good idea if the vehicle is used only on the road as it will lower the comfortable cruising speed and raise petrol consumption, though of course acceleration will be improved. But if competition is the object, this lowering of the overall gearing is a very worthwhile improvement, especially for sprints, hill climbs and most of the tight English circuits. The actual ratio chosen will depend very much on individual taste, as well as trial and error, but a rough guide is that the 4.1:1 ratio should be used for short, against-the-clock events and circuits like Brands Hatch Club, while the 3.9:1 ratio is very useful for circuits like Goodwood. As the range of available final-drive assemblies has widened, some people, particularly with 850 Minis, have gone for very low overall gearing, taking the ratio as far as 4.6:1. However, I think this lowers the gearing too far, and in my opinion 4.1:1 or at most 4.3:1 are still ideal for most circuits.

One other transmission modification involves fitting the Cooper S optional limited-slip differential which may be worthwhile on the 850 Mini depending on the intended use, and is essential for out-and-out competition. It accentuates the throttle-sensitive nature of the car's handling, to say the least, and will not reward the clumsy driver!

Up till mid-1969, the limited-slip differential used in most racers were designed for use with the standard or 'standard equivalent' crown wheels. Since then, a Salisbury limited-slip unit has become common which requires a special crown wheel. The pinion pattern remains unaltered.

7

Suspension, brakes and body

There are two types of Mini suspension, solid rubber and Hydrolastic, and they call for different approaches to modification. The basic design uses rubber cones under compression as the springing medium, linked to the suspension arms or wishbones by alloy or steel trumpet-shaped struts. The solid rubber version has conventional telescopic shock absorbers, while the Hydrolastic version has damping properties designed into the system of fluid interconnection between front and rear.

Beginning with the solid rubber type, most people will find that it needs improvement when the car is tuned for greater performance, particularly because of the inefficiency of the standard shock absorbers and the high ride setting which together can cause wallowing and pitching when cornering hard under power. The priority is to fit decent shock absorbers which should not only be double acting and heavy duty but should also preferably be adjustable. They are easily fitted and widely available from tuning shops.

For a long time, I personally always used Konis as they have excellent damping qualities and have also proved to be very long-lasting: even when they begin to weaken, adjusting them to a stiffer setting will prolong their usefulness. I have also found Armstrong Adjustarides to be very good, and they have the advantage that they can be adjusted without taking them off the car, which is particularly useful at the back and if you want to make changes in a hurry. There are also a number of other reputable makes on the market.

Shock absorber settings will be determined by personal preference as a matter of trial and error, but I have always found them best when the front is set hard and the rear left at medium – as compared with standard dampers which are soft all round.

The solid rubber Mini suspension is simplicity itself to lower. All one needs to do is to machine or carefully hacksaw an appropriate amount off the ball-joint end of the alloy or steel trumpet mentioned earlier. Because of the geometry of leverage in the suspension, small amounts removed from the trumpets lower the car quite a lot: if you want to reduce the height by, say, 2in you certainly don't take 2in off the trumpets! The ratio of the amount to be taken off the trumpet relative to the consequent lowering of the car is approximately 3:1 at the front and 5:1 at the rear.

That means that every $\frac{1}{16}$in cut off the struts lowers the car by about $\frac{3}{16}$in at the front and $\frac{5}{16}$in at the rear. Many Minis have $\frac{1}{16}$in-thick wire washers inserted between the end of the trumpet and the shoulder of the steel ball. These should be removed, but remember that this is the same as cutting $\frac{1}{16}$in off the strut.

It is difficult to be specific about the amount of lowering necessary because individual Minis all seem to vary in their ride height anyway. I always aim to leave about $\frac{1}{2}$in between the bottom of the wing edge and the top of the tyre at the front and about 1$\frac{1}{4}$in at the rear. It does however depend on individual choice and the use to which the vehicle is to be put, and it may be best to lower the car by stages until you find what suits you (remembering that the process is not reversible without buying new trumpets!). When cutting the trumpets, care should be taken to see that the resulting surface mates up squarely and evenly with the shoulder of the ball which is a push-fit in the trumpet.

There are two limitations on how far you can lower a Mini. The first obvious limit is that if lowered too far the wheelarches will foul the tyres, especially at the rear and when using wider wheels and/or fatter tyres. This can be overcome by bodywork modifications like cutting the front wings away and raising the rear arches by cutting and rewelding.

The second and final limit, which cannot be overcome, involves the design of the suspension. The trumpet ball fits into a cup on either the front wishbone or the rear swinging arm, and only the fact that the rubber suspension unit remains compressed keeps the ball in place. If the car is lowered too far, the balls are liable to come out of the cups when the suspension is in the full rebound position and the suspension will then collapse!

Some people stipulate that when a Mini is lowered to somewhere near the limit, special short shock absorbers should be used to prevent them bottoming and consequently suffering rapid wear or damage. I personally do not like these short dampers because in my experience their short travel accentuates the tendency to lift a rear wheel when cornering hard, especially in racing conditions. Also I have never known the suspension to bottom with the car in racing trim

and just the driver on board, so the danger of damage to the dampers seems very slight and a little extra wear is acceptable under the circumstances. It does depend on the degree of lowering, though. For road use, for example, when passengers may very well be carried, the short dampers may be essential: if the suspension does repeatedly bottom it will quickly suffer damage and will sooner or later break one or other of the mounting points. One suspension modification which should definitely not be carried out on a solid rubber 850 Mini is the fitting of a rear anti-roll bar.

The Hydrolastic suspension system is rather less amenable to simple modification, having no external dampers to be changed. There is a tension spring where the rear damper fits on the 'dry' version. Also, from what I have seen, the standard ride height is quite low enough for most purposes. This suspension is more sensitive to ride height, though, and a car that rides too high will tend to roll badly.

There have been some changes in production affecting parts fitted to cars with Hydrolastic suspension, and it is advisable to use the correctly matched components as they are basically not interchangeable. Early Hydrolastic cars had suspension units to one specification across the range, without any special identification. Colour coding was applied to the alternative stiffer units available for some territories. After the changes, the units for ordinary Mini and Mini Cooper models were identified by orange bands, while

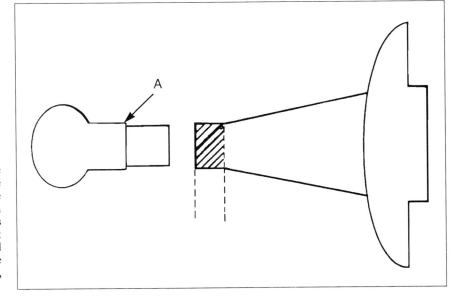

Mini suspension of the solid rubber type can be lowered by removing the appropriate amount from the end of the trumpet, as shown shaded. The cut must be square and smooth so that the shoulder of the ball, A, seats properly.

those for the Cooper S were competition specification units with blue bands. Concurrently with these changes, the rear helper springs and rear struts were changed too, the later parts being numbers 21A 1806 and 21A 1805 respectively.

For an early car, the biggest improvement comes from fitting the later Hydrolastic units. This not only stiffens the suspension and hence lessens roll but also reduces the tendency for the car to wander from a straight line at high speed.

Refer to the workshop manual for full details of dismantling and re-assembling the Hydrolastic suspension if you are not already familiar with this unconventional system. After fitting new displacer units, ensure that the struts remain located in the ball sockets at the start of pressurizing. Take the pressure up to 350psi and wait at least 30 minutes for the vehicle to settle before reducing to the correct running pressure. These pressures are high enough to cause damage or injury in the event of equipment failure, so do not use improvised apparatus: if in doubt, get a properly equipped agent to undertake the depressurizing and repressurizing.

The Hydrolastic system incorporates internal damping, so the fitting of additional shock absorbers is not normally recommended. There is, however, a factory shock absorber kit for rallying (part number C-AJJ 3362).

If the tendency of the front end of the car to rise under fierce acceleration is a problem, this may be remedied by fitting larger, progressive rear bump stops, available as a complete set (part number C-AJJ 3313). These will also help to improve the handling of the car when the rear is heavily laden.

The ride height can be raised if required to increase ground clearance by fitting spacer washers to the struts, but excessive packing can be dangerous and under no circumstances should a washer thicker than 0.15in (3.8mm) be fitted. To compensate for extra weight on the front end such as a sump guard and rallying lamps, earlier cars can be fitted with the later, stronger rear helper spring. Only limited ride height adjustment is possible by altering the pressure in the Hydrolastic system: cars should not be run with the pressure exceeding 300psi. As well as affecting the handling, damage will result if the car is driven while making continual contact with the rebound stops. An accurate pressure gauge is essential.

For circuit racing on smooth tracks, the suspension of earlier Hydrolastic cars may be lowered by accurately machining 0.2in from the front strut and 0.3in from the rear strut. Before refitting these parts it is essential to check that the ball sockets still seat properly, if necessary by filing to remove any ridges. Do not use the standard rear bump stops: fit the uprated progressive stops already mentioned or, if they are considered to provide too much stiffness, use part numbers 21A 1728 and 21A 1729 with the special securing screws and washers of the uprated type. Pack the rebound stops to compensate for the lowering of the car, so ensuring that suspension movement remains controlled. An adjustable anti-roll bar kit is available which may be useful in fine-tuning the handling of a Hydrolastic car.

After allowing new displacer units to settle, the pressure can be lowered until the car is just clear of the bump stops. Note that the car will settle lower when the fluid is cold, and do not run with pressures below 220psi. It does not matter if the pressures are uneven from side to side, it is more important that the height should be the same.

With either suspension system, adding negative camber at both front and rear wheels can give useful gains in roadholding, but the amount will depend very much on personal preference and on other aspects of how the car is set up. Details are included in the Cooper S chapter.

The steering of the Mini needs no attention, except to ensure that it is in good order, and perhaps to lower the upper end of the column a little to improve the driving position, as detailed at the end of this chapter. The later steering rack, part number 21A196 for right-hand drive or 21A1962 for left-hand drive, should be used on all rally, autocross or rallycross cars.

Wheels and spacers
The wheel track can easily be increased by fitting spacers of a reputable type, or at the rear by using Cooper S rear drums which have a built-in spacer. Fitting wheel spacers will necessitate fitting longer studs too. I would limit any track increase to 1in as the leverage exerted on the wheel studs is greatly increased and becomes unsafe above this amount. If the studs break the wheels drop off – quite possibly without warning!

If using spacers or Cooper S drums, the stronger Cooper S 4½in wheels can be used, in themselves a very useful improvement. There is also the so-called 'reversed rim' Cooper S wheel, originally produced by Dunlop's wheel division, still with a 4½in rim but giving 1in greater track increase than the standard Cooper S wheel. This is very useful because it can be used without a spacer, thus reducing unsprung weight. Wheelarch extensions then become necessary to cover the tyre completely, and most tuning specialists have a variety on offer.

One problem often associated with the use of spacers and wide-rim wheels is excessively rapid wear of the wheel bearings. Converting to the Cooper S-type taper-roller bearings means changing a lot of other parts too, and I have found that simply using a molybdenum-rich grease solves the problem perfectly well, with no signs of wear in the ordinary bearings on my Mini after a season and a half of circuit racing.

Braking improvements
The standard Mini brake linings in my opinion are useless for repeated slowing from high speed, and greatly need improving on any car tuned for additional performance. The Minis that preceded the 1964 Motor Show had single-leading-shoe front brakes: after that date the friction area was increased slightly and a twin-leading-shoe arrangement introduced.

The first and most obvious improvement to either type is to fit better brake linings. The standard front linings, originally Ferodo AM3 specification, should be replaced by Ferodo AM4 or an equivalent, leaving the rear linings standard. On an early Mini it may well pay to fit the newer larger shoes, if not using Cooper S rear drums. On the other hand, if money is no object, you may wish to fit front discs: if so, do not use any other type than Cooper S, but remember that this will involve fitting whole new Cooper S front assemblies and can be expensive. In my opinion, the drums are quite adequate for an 850 – and certainly better than Cooper (non-S) discs.

I would be very much inclined to convert a later Mini back to the single-leading-shoe type at the front. In my experience, the later, twin-leading-shoe arrangement has always been far more prone to the bad effects of fade than the original pattern. There is some theoretical basis for this, too, ably explained in the technical literature on the subject. Suffice to say here that with twin leading shoes a 25% decrease in lining efficiency can result in a decrease of 50% or more in overall braking efficiency.

Do not fit a servo. I think they are a waste of money on this particular car, unless one has a problem with a weak leg. In fact I actively hate boosters on Minis since I have found that they tend to accentuate brake grab and hang on after

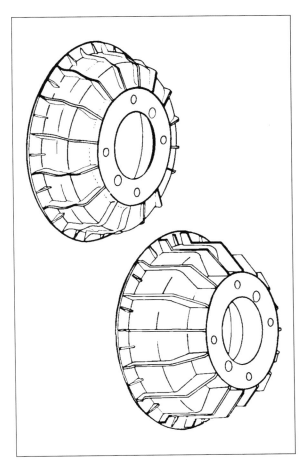

Minifin replacement brake drums are light alloy with cast-in iron inserts for the friction area. They provide better heat dissipation for reduced fade, and also lower unsprung weight. One type (lower) has an integral spacer, Cooper S style.

the pedal has been released; this even applies to the standard fitting on the Cooper S. Remember that with a powerful, front-wheel-drive car, braking is extremely important and, especially when racing, there is nothing more embarrassing than leaving braking to the last moment, jumping on the brakes and then finding that they grab or hang on for a fraction too long as you go into a corner. The net result can be an inverted and bent Mini!

The improved version of the Minifin replacement brake drum, in light alloy with an iron insert, is a very worthwhile fitting. I have used them on my racing 850 Mini, front and rear, and would not be without them. Besides improving braking because they reduce fade through better heat dissipation, they give the additional bonuses of reduced unsprung weight and longer brake lining life. AM4 linings used with standard all-iron brake drums had a racing life of approximately 150 miles: with Minifin drums, the linings were still good after some 400 miles of racing.

It may be worthwhile cutting louvres in the front valance under the bumper in an effort to increase the flow of cold air to the front brakes. When racing, removal of the front flasher units can also help towards this.

Bodywork modifications
The first Minis, 1959 and early 1960 models, had lighter but less robust bodyshells than later versions. The weight difference was about 40lb. For competition, weight reduction is all-important. What is possible may very well be tightly controlled by the particular set of regulations to which you will be subject, so check carefully before you start throwing out superfluous trim, seats or other fittings!

The first and most important modification, rules permitting, is to replace the rear and side windows with Perspex, the thickness of which will depend on whether you are prepared to do without sealing rubbers or not. The thinnest practical Perspex can be screwed into place and sealed with Bostic or some similar rubbery compound. However, competition rules do insist that the windows must remain rigid and this does impose a limitation on how thin the Perspex can be. In some cases there is a fire resistance requirement too, which will call for a higher specification material.

But if the glass can be replaced by a plastic material of some kind, the weight saving is quite considerable. It also lowers the vehicle's centre of gravity a little, to the benefit of handling and roadholding. The front screen can be replaced by $\frac{3}{16}$in or $\frac{1}{4}$in Perspex, again rules permitting, but in this case one must be prepared to keep burnishing scratches out of the surface or vision very quickly becomes impaired, and I would not recommend such a modification except as an extreme measure for racing.

All internal trim and mats can easily be removed, together with unnecessary items like the heater, chrome trim, ashtrays, etc: even the speedo can be discarded under some racing

regulations. Ideally, the bonnet, bootlid and doors can be replaced by lighter panels made of glassfibre or aluminium. However, if money is a limiting factor, access to a good breaker's yard is very useful because slightly bent panels can be obtained very cheaply and straightened quite well with a bit of care. Then the inner skin or strengthening strips, including the door pockets, can be cut away, and you can cut out the main part of the outer steel panel and replace it with thin aluminium sheet pop-riveted in place. This can be done quite cheaply and is most effective.

Personally, I would never use all-glassfibre doors because I think that the steel frames of the standard doors add considerably to the strength of the car if it rolls over. I would always just cut away the door pocket and replace the main panel with aluminium. The bonnet and bootlid, however, can be replaced with glassfibre, either bought ready-made or fabricated using the originals as moulds. The biggest problem with that operation is ensuring that the glassfibre does not stick to the mould panel, and to prevent this a first layer of greasy newspaper over the steel mould is a good idea. Further weight can be saved by dispensing with the bonnet and boot locks, using Dzus fasteners or leather straps in their place.

I would not recommend significant lightening of any other body panels since Minis rely very much on their integral unit construction for strength and rigidity. Any structural lightening can not only seriously affect the roadholding and handling because of flexing, it can also result in the complete break-up of the bodyshell, especially in the event of even a minor shunt, with consequences too horrible to contemplate.

The comfort of the Mini driving position can be greatly improved by fitting a proprietary bucket seat (essential for almost any form of competition) and by using special brackets, available from most accessory shops or Mini tuning specialists, to lower the steering column by about an inch at its dash mounting. First slacken the four Nyloc nuts just beneath the front bulkhead inside the car: these clamp the rack in position, and loosening them enables the rack and column to be rotated into the required position. Do not forget to retighten them when the column brackets have been fitted. This modification has no adverse effects whatsoever on the vehicle.

8

The 998cc engine

The 998cc version of the Mini power unit first appeared in the Riley Elf and Wolseley Hornet and then was later made available in the ordinary saloons and estate cars. It has the bore dimension of the Austin/Morris 1100 engine combined with the stroke of the A-series engine in its 948cc form familiar in cars like the Morris 1000 and earlier Sprites. These dimensions are shared with the second Cooper which replaced the first, long-stroke 997cc version, but that engine has other differences which are explained in the next chapter. The 998 Mini has a remote gearchange instead of the 850's 'magic wand', an improvement shared with most later Mini derivatives.

While the 970cc version of the Cooper S is the ultimate Mini for the up-to-1,000cc class in competition, the 998 can be useful for less extreme forms of motorsport or as a good basis for a brisk road car. In the latter role, it certainly makes more sense than trying to overbore an 850 for increased capacity.

It is not possible to fit the 998 crankshaft straight into an 850 block as the crankshaft webs are thicker and it would entail reducing the width of the centre main-bearing housing. The standard 998 pistons have a 6cc dish and this would make it difficult to use them in a full-race engine where the aim is a compression ratio of something like 12:1.

The 998 block is identical to the 1100 block. Later ones were strengthened slightly in comparison to the earliest version, but this has little relevance to any but the perfectionist because I have never known early 998/1100

blocks to give trouble, nor have I heard any such reports from the major tuning companies, having checked this point with them.

The head on the 998 engine is slightly better than that on the 850, but the differences are so slight that I would not really consider this head to be a worthwhile tuning aid like the 12G295 casting used on 998 Coopers and MG 1100s is. The standard 998 head can be modified in exactly the same way as that of the 850, but because of the larger capacity, enlarged valves produce a much more worthwhile improvement even for fast road use. Here again the Cooper, or better still MG 1100, inlet valve should be used. Finances permitting, I would always fit the complete Cooper or MG 1100 head which, in basic form, is of superior design to either the 850 or standard 998 components. Modification of that head is covered later.

Good results can be obtained using the standard (though modified) inlet manifold and a single carburettor, as detailed for the 850 engine. In this case I would not use larger inlet valves than those fitted to the standard Cooper. However, because of its increased capacity again, the 998 engine is far better able to utilize the improved breathing offered by twin carburettors and a special inlet manifold. For fast road use, and when tuning on a modest budget, excellent results can come from using the standard Cooper/Cooper S set-up, with twin 1¼in SU HS2 carburettors and light alloy manifold. If petrol consumption is not too important, twin

1½in SU H4 carburettors, or a single 45 DCOE Weber, will give more ultimate performance.

The standard Cooper/Cooper S exhaust manifold is both cheap and very efficient, though some may prefer to fit the products of the specialist tuning firms. The effectiveness of these unfortunately too often varies, and while some are good, others are just expensive replicas of the standard BMC product. For this engine I would certainly recommend using the standard Cooper exhaust pipe and silencer (suitably lengthened in the case of the longer-bodied Traveller, Elf or Hornet): it is of larger diameter throughout than the standard 850/998 system.

The camshaft housing has liner bearings as standard so a higher-performance camshaft can be fitted with no other modifications save for the obvious lightening of the valve gear. Ideal choices are the standard Cooper or C-AEA 731 camshafts, which on this engine give excellent top-end performance coupled with good bottom-end torque for road use. If racing is envisaged, the 544 or even 648 camshaft can be used. In the latter case, the high-lift profile of the cam makes it necessary to machine out the spring-locating grooves, fit the longer springs from the Cooper S and possibly also sink the valve seats deeper into the head, otherwise the springs will crush at full lift with consequent dire results. In all cases where an improved camshaft is fitted, it is worthwhile also fitting the Hidural bronze-alloy valve guides used as standard on the Cooper S. They last longer and minimize the danger of seizure at high revs. Remember again to match the distributor, or more specifically its advance curve, to the camshaft being used.

As higher bearing and crankshaft loads will result from the larger capacity of this engine, it is essential to strengthen the centre main-bearing cap for competition use and engine speeds above 7,000rpm. This can be done by fitting a specially machined steel replacement cap or by giving the standard component the support of a steel strap, as detailed earlier.

This engine has the advantage of being basically stronger than that of the 850 Mini, principally because it is fitted with fully floating connecting rods so that the danger of engine failure resulting from gudgeon-pin clamp bolt failure is eliminated. Suitably modified, a 998 engine originating from an ordinary Mini can be tuned in exactly the same way as a 998 Cooper unit.

It is possible to increase the capacity of the 998 engine to over 1,100cc by boring the block and using the long-stroke crankshaft of the earlier, 997cc Cooper along with special pistons. Several tuning companies have offered this conversion, but I can see little point because it is not cheap and is likely to decrease the engine's reliability. Other things, such as the availability of suitable parts, being equal, a better result can be achieved by using the 1,071cc Cooper S engine, clutch, flywheel and cylinder head. This can be grafted on to the existing gearbox with little difficulty: it may be necessary to relieve parts of the inside of the gearbox casing with a hand file to prevent the crankshaft fouling, but the areas in which this is required are easily apparent to the eye of even a novice tuner if he offers the engine up to the gearbox before attempting assembly.

9

Mini-Cooper

The 997cc and 998cc Coopers are in most respects very similar in specification and degree of tune, the only real difference being in the detail structure of the engine. The 997cc Cooper, which was the earlier version, had a relatively long-throw crankshaft, giving it a long stroke with a fairly narrow bore dimension. The pistons were not of the flat-top type, and the little ends had clamp bolts on the connecting rods to retain the gudgeon pins. The very early examples had an oilway drilled in the tail end of the crankshaft beneath the primary gear. The crank was, however, stronger than that of the early 850 Minis and was fitted with a vibration damper at the front (pulley) end to prevent timing-chain breakage.

The 998cc Cooper, which replaced the earlier type in January 1964, has a larger bore and shorter stroke. The pistons are virtually flat topped and the little ends are fully floating, the gudgeon pins being a light press fit in the connecting rods and retained in the pistons by circlips. The earlier car had its own cylinder head, the first of several improvements on the basic Mini head design which were to appear over the years, while the 998cc version has a slightly different head (casting 12G 295) shared with the engine of the MG 1100. This later Cooper engine has proved stronger and more reliable than the earlier type. Apart from the pistons, crankshaft damper, camshaft, cylinder head and manifolds, it is identical to the 998cc unit used in ordinary Minis, Elves and Hornets.

These differences apart, the two Coopers can be treated as identical and the tuning procedures are much the same, except that the clamp-bolt connecting rods of the earlier engine should be replaced by the later type, as already described for the 850 Mini. Although I referred to the 998 Cooper pistons as 'flat topped', in point of fact they have a crown slightly raised in the centre, and a worthwhile improvement would be to change them for slightly dished pistons, though this may not be practical. If not, it would be easier simply to machine them flat: flat pistons are, in my opinion, better than the raised-crown type.

Standard Cooper equipment includes twin SU HS2 1¼in carburettors on a cast light-alloy inlet manifold fitted with a balance pipe, and a free-flow long-branch exhaust manifold leading to a large-diameter exhaust pipe. Other Cooper advantages include the fact that the cylinder head (either type) is fitted with larger inlet valves than the basic Mini, and is cast to a shape similar to, if not better than, the shape one aims for when modifying the ordinary 850 cylinder head. The valves are fitted with stronger springs. The oil pump is heavier duty and longer lasting than the early 850 type. The clutch has stronger springs and the gearbox contains slightly closer ratios, selected by the remote-control type gearchange. Disc brakes are fitted at the front, although they are very small and pretty useless.

Cylinder head
The basic principles of cylinder head modification are exactly the same as for the less highly tuned Mini engines, but since much of the

basic shaping work has been done by the manufacturer it is possible to go a stage further without the danger of breaking through into oilways or the water jacket.

For instance, it is possible with the 997cc head to remove almost completely the beak in the combustion chamber to relieve valve masking. The inlet port is already cast with a rectangular shape and can be smoothed out and possibly enlarged a little in exactly the same way as on the ordinary Mini head. The same procedure as before also applies to the valve throats, the valves themselves and the seats.

Because of the larger capacity of this engine, the ports and valves can be enlarged more than those of an 850 with advantage, although, as before, it is possible to go too far, with counter-productive results. If larger valves are to be fitted to an earlier Cooper then the obvious choice is to use the standard MG 1100 inlet valve – or better still fit the even better MG 1100 cylinder head complete, as the manufacturers did with the 998c Cooper. That head is covered later in the book.

Even on this engine, I still feel that there is no point in enlarging the exhaust valves, or for that matter wasting a lot of time on modifying the exhaust ports or valves.

Carburettors and manifolds

There seems to me little point in replacing the existing standard manifolds, unless you are prepared to do a lot of swapping and experiment, since many specialist manifolds show no improvement whatsoever, while many others show only marginal improvements and then only over certain parts of the rev range. However, the standard inlet manifold should of course be carefully gas-flowed and lightly polished internally.

A useful increase in power can be found by replacing the 1¼in carburettors with 1½in H4 SUs. As always, the precise set-up of the carburettors will depend on the extent of modifications on any particular engine, but a good starting point in this case is CP4 needles, blue springs and fast-lift vacuum chambers, together with competition jets and needle valves. The dashpots should be filled with thin lubricating oil such as '3-in-1'. New H4 carburettors already set up to this specification were available direct from SU, but a possible and cheaper alternative is to buy second-hand and carry out your own modifications.

When fitting twin 1½in carburettors, the inlet manifold must be suitably modified by opening out the holes at the carburettor flanges. In this case the enlarging should be carried out equally all round the diameter of the opening, not offset to the top as with the 850 Mini manifold.

Some people claim that a 45 DCOE Weber on a suitable special manifold gives even better results, but this is debatable and there is much conflicting evidence. Experiment by all means if you have the money: if not, stick to SUs.

Camshafts

The 997 Cooper has the 2A948 camshaft as standard, whereas the 998 Cooper is fitted with the AEH 148 camshaft (the same as the 630 for most practical purposes) and a useful tuning aid is to replace it with the 2A948 type. Hotter replacements with competition in mind might be the C-AEA 731 for road/sprint use or the 544 camshaft for racing. As explained before, it is possible to fit the AEA 648 or 649 camshaft, given the necessary modifications to accommodate the extra lift and avoid spring crush.

Braking system

Although at first sight it would appear that the brakes on the Cooper are superior to those of ordinary Minis, because there are discs at the front, in practice this is not so. Most people have found that when really hard-pressed, particularly under competitive conditions, these brakes are worse than useless, even when modified, snatching and pulling to one side on the first few applications and thereafter fading away almost completely. One well known racing driver, when asked one day at Brands Hatch, 'What are the brakes like?' replied, 'What brakes? I didn't think it had any. But still, who uses brakes on these things anyway?'

Various modifications have been tried, including servos which don't help. Better linings and pads (such as Ferodo DS 11 front and VG 95 rear) and larger calipers are the best that can be done. Ducting cold air to the brakes can help, too. If these measures are not enough, more extreme solutions are to revert to drum brakes or fit the complete Cooper S assemblies including drive-shafts. Drums are much the cheaper method but not the best: at least they can be persuaded to behave fairly consistently.

The problem with the ordinary Cooper is that the discs are too small and consequently overheat. Even on the Cooper S the disc size is limited by the small wheel size, and cooling is hampered by the shrouding effect of the wheel on the brake friction area. Progress in pad materials, though, has helped to reduce the problem over the years.

Lydden Hill again. The rigours of rallycross combined with drastic weight-saving measures often produce partial disintegration – with no loss of speed!

Mo Mendham, saloon racing at Brands Hatch, presses on with unabated vigour despite the handicap of a semi-detached bonnet.

59

10

1100 and other A-series

The BMC A-series engine is of course found in a whole range of vehicles other than the Mini, and both tuning techniques and specific components are interchangeable to varying degrees between them. Most closely related to the Mini by virtue of the fact that their engine and transmission assemblies are almost identical are the Austin and Morris 1100 cars, and their MG, Wolseley and Riley derivatives. Because they have never caught the imagination of the enthusiast to anywhere near the same extent as the Mini, much less attention has been paid to them by the tuning specialists, but a good deal of Mini lore is directly applicable. The gearbox and clutch, for example, can be treated in exactly the same way. An exception is the braking system: the modifications suggested for the ordinary Cooper brakes apply, but fitting Cooper S units is not possible in this case.

It is the engine department which offers the most obvious opportunities for improvement, and tuning can follow exactly the same lines as for the Mini. These models already have the fully floating little ends and camshaft bearing liners which are required as improvements to the basic Mini. The very earliest Morris 1100s had very weak gudgeon pins, but this was rectified under warranty (by changing the pins, connecting rods and pistons) and it is unlikely that any are still at large.

The carburation and manifolds of the Austin and Morris 1100s are very similar to those used on the 850 Mini and can thus be treated in exactly the same manner. The MG 1100 (like the Riley and Wolseley versions) has a twin-

carburettor set-up very similar to the 997/998 Coopers. So all modifications in this field are exactly as previously described, though the type of needle finally chosen for the carburettor/s is likely to be different because of the engine's greater capacity, and for the same reason the benefits of using twin carburettors will be proportionally greater than with an 848cc unit.

The exhaust manifold on the MG 1100 is slightly different from that fitted to the Cooper in that it has shorter branches and a smaller diameter outlet. Thus it may be worthwhile experimenting with the use of a standard Cooper exhaust manifold. It is of course the smaller outlet of the MG 1100 manifold which makes it particularly suitable for use on an 850 Mini where an increase in exhaust pipe diameter is undesirable.

The cylinder head on the basic Austin/Morris 1100 models displays most of the features already discussed in relation to the ordinary Mini engine. The MG 1100 head, however, is of more advanced design, which makes it a useful tuning aid, as already suggested. As with the other A-series heads, the design is based on the venerable Weslake cylinder head with heart-shaped combustion chamber, the beak of which prevents heat transference between the hot exhaust valve and the cooler inlet valve. As before, there are three exhaust ports and two siamesed inlet ports. But this head displays in standard form most of the modifications previously suggested for other models, with the exception of the valve seats, guides, bosses and throats. It has, however, only a rough cast finish, as with many mass-produced heads. The valves are larger than for any of the Mini models except the Cooper S, but the inlet ports, though of square section, are even smaller than on the Cooper.

Although the first MG 1100 head represented a considerable improvement on the original Mini design, there have been even further developments. After much research, BMC and their cylinder head experts came up with a very shallow head for this engine, giving greatly improved gas flow and better burning characteristics. So, with the exception of the Cooper S component, this 12G 295 casting represents the ultimate standard production A-series head.

Further improvement is possible along the lines already described, because the enthusiast can

earliest form, pre-1957, with a capacity of only 803cc, it had very little reserve of strength to withstand tuning, but the first increase in capacity, to 948cc, was accompanied by some beefing-up of basic components like the crankshaft, and that version of the engine was one of the most widely used.

The 948cc unit is very similar to the Mini engine and in some respects identical, many parts being interchangeable. The main difference is in the crankshaft, flywheel and clutch assembly, because of the different transmission arrangements. The connecting rods have clamp-bolts at the little ends, and the camshaft runs direct in the block without bearing liners. The cylinder head can be taken to nearly the same point as that of the Mini for tuning purposes, but some examples may be found to have less solid

Though closely related to the Mini in engineering, the Austin and Morris 1100, and later the 1300, never achieved anything remotely like the same sort of reputation. Their existence widened the range of available engines, though.

always dedicate more time and effort to the job than is feasible in mass production, but the gains will of course be proportionally less because the starting point is further along the road. There is little point in trying to increase the valve size. I would suggest a compression ratio of between 10:1 and 11:1, with a rev limit of 6,500 to 7,000rpm. Achieving a sufficiently high compression ratio, particularly for racing, may mean machining through the horizontal oilway close to the head face, but this can be repaired by brazing in a suitable pipe.

Longitudinal A-series
Apart from its use in transverse-mounted form in BMC's front-wheel-drive cars, the A-series engine has of course powered numerous conventional, rear-drive models such as the Austin A30, A35 and A40, the Morris Minor and 1000, and the Sprite/Midget sports cars. In its

metal in them, limiting the possible extent of machining and reshaping.

The capacity can be increased to 997cc, and in fact the 998 Cooper specification is a good starting point for serious tuning of this engine, including fitting the Cooper or MG 1100 cylinder head. Camshaft bearing liners, 998 or 1100 pattern fully-floating connecting rods and flat-top pistons are required, and then tuning can proceed as for the Cooper, remembering that the Cooper's 948 camshaft is a useful performance extra on these cars, the standard camshaft having very mild timing. Modifications to the valve gear are exactly as for the Mini.

For racing with this engine, there is one essential addition to all the normal tuning mods and that is to fit the special steel crankshaft (part number C-AEA 406) because the standard crankshaft is sure to fracture under the stress of continual high revs. The clutch is another

61

The works team Cooper S cars had a tremendously successful rallying career in the 1960s in the hands of drivers like Timo Makinen, Rauno Aaltonen, Paddy Hopkirk and Simo Lampinen.

weakness as it tends to break up under such extreme conditions, and it should be replaced by the competition coil-spring clutch or, better but more expensive, a special diaphragm-spring clutch unit complete with new flywheel. Thus tuned, this motor can be safely revved to 8,000rpm and it makes a very good little competition engine, developing something like 85bhp – some people claim up to 100bhp!

The next development with the production A-series engine in its lengthways-mounted form was a longer stroke, increasing the capacity to 1,098cc: this unit is very close to that of the Morris 1100, with similar connecting rods and camshaft housing. Austin and Morris versions have a cylinder head just like that of the transverse 1100, while the Sprite/Midget version sports a Cooper or MG 1100 type head, together with a hotter camshaft. Unfortunately there are no special crankshafts available and consequently, fully tuned, this engine is not as reliable or high-revving as a fully tuned 948cc unit. It has thus rarely been used for competition. A later version for the Sprite and Midget was strengthened by increasing the main-bearing journal diameter to 2in, but it is still not as strong as the steel crankshaft. Special clutches are again available for this unit, and essential for use at sustained high revs.

In each case, the techniques applicable to

tuning the Mini engine can be extended to these other A-series units, and the underlying principles remain the same. The ultimate development of the engine, in both transverse and lengthways form, took it to 1,275cc, adopting the capacity but not all the other features of the big Cooper S: more details in Chapter 12.

Outside the mainstream of production A-series engines there were some special competition units. One of the first was the 1,098cc Formula Junior engine. This had a block very similar to the 948cc, but with strengthened main bearings. It had stronger connecting rods, special timing gear and camshaft, and a cylinder head which was more or less a cross between the Cooper and Cooper S heads, having 11 studs but bore centres the same as the Cooper. There were quite a lot of these around and they were ideal, for example, for a racing Sprite. But the special components, and in particular the connecting rods, were very expensive to replace if they got broken.

The other principal competition A-series engine was a direct derivative of the Cooper S, adapted for longitudinal mounting with a suitable crankshaft and flywheel. It came in 970 and 1,275cc varieties, but it was very difficult to get the manufacturers to admit to its existence and a great deal of arm-twisting and persistence was needed to get hold of one!

11

Mini-Cooper S

The Cooper S differs so much in detail from the more basic Minis, including the ordinary Cooper, that it needs to be dealt with separately. The same underlying principles of tuning apply, of course, but the S is mechanically stronger in almost every respect and so in general needs much less of the substitution of components which is required with the lesser models simply to achieve durability. Almost every weakness discovered on tuned Minis and Coopers has been rectified in the S model.

Some of the ideas and modifications which will be suggested for the Cooper S can be adapted to suit the more mundane Mini variants, but that increased strength factor must be borne in mind: in some cases what may be ideal for the S could cause serious mechanical failure on other models. So proceed with caution, think the modifications through carefully first and, if in doubt, consult an expert – it could save you a great deal of time and money.

The first Cooper S was the 1071 version, with an engine based on experience gained in Formula Junior single-seaters (hence the nominal 1,100cc capacity), and about 4,000 were produced between March 1960 and August 1964. Two other versions appeared in March 1964: the 970 was intended purely to secure homologation in the up-to-1,000cc class for competition, was available only to special order, for less than a year, and reached a production total of less than 1,000 examples. The 1275 was by far the most numerous (total production over 20,000) and is the model most people immediately think of when you say 'Cooper S'.

I am going to treat the three different versions as one model for most purposes since tuning procedures are basically the same: where there is a difference it will be explained. The Cooper S can be regarded as an out-and-out competition version of the Mini-Cooper, with almost every specialist tuning technique already incorporated by the manufacturer. The main exceptions are hand finishing of the cylinder head, and the inlet valve seats which came off the production line wider than necessary and cut at 45 degrees. Because these cars were sold to the general public, they have relatively mild camshaft profiles, low compression ratio and small carburettors in the interests of good road manners in traffic and reasonable fuel economy.

There have been few changes to the Cooper S specification in the course of production, apart from the obvious alterations shared with the whole Mini range such as Hydrolastic suspension and the adoption of diaphragm-spring clutches, and only three or four will concern the tuning enthusiast. Early cars were very prone to overheating when driven really hard, especially under competitive conditions. This was found to be due to the cylinder head which had inadequate cooling characteristics, and that first design, known as the 'yellow' head, was eventually replaced by the 'blue' head, which not only cools better but is incidentally of superior design for tuning and sets very little limit to the amount which can be machined off to raise the compression ratio.

After the 1967 Motor Show, the cylinder head studs were superseded by a new type made of stronger, high-tensile material. Part numbers are 51K275 (long) and 51K276 (short). These studs, which permit a tightening torque of 45lb/ft, can be identified by their black colour and a small dimple punched in the top end.

The other changes concerned the front suspension assembly. The steering arms linking the rack to the hubs were considerably beefed-up in diameter for additional strength, and the front hubs were altered in detail in an effort to prevent the rapid wear of wheel bearings which many people were experiencing.

The 970 engine suffers, especially in tuned form, from lack of torque at low revs. It can, however, be safely revved to 8,000rpm and I know of people who have regularly used 9,000 or even 10,000rpm. In the latter case, though, all the valve gear and reciprocating parts are extensively lightened, even to the extent of making some components of different materials such as titanium alloy. The 1071 is a good average engine, with reasonable torque and the ability to rev safely to 8,000rpm or just over. It does show a slight tendency to overheat under extreme conditions but this normally only manifests itself when racing in hot weather.

The 1275 engine has an amazing amount of torque at low revs even when tuned, and yet it can safely be taken up to nearly 8,000rpm, though I would put the limit at 7,300 to 7,500rpm for regular use. In fact, with a good close-ratio gearbox, it is unnecessary to exceed these engine speeds in the intermediate gears, because of the excellent torque, leaving ultra-high revs for extreme circumstances only. This engine does, however, have two unpleasant faults: it tends to overheat and it knocks its bearings out rather quickly.

The overheating is basically due to the longer stroke, with its inherent greater friction, and also the fact that the engine is slightly taller to accommodate this stroke, the extra height taking the form of extra, largely uncooled, metal at the top of the block compared with the smaller-capacity versions. The side-radiator layout inherited from the basic Mini doesn't allow much leeway for coping with the inevitably greater heat output of a larger-capacity engine, either. A new high-output water pump has been introduced to combat the cooling problems experienced on some highly developed racing engines. This will fit all A-series engines, though in some cases it may be necessary to remove casting marks from the block inside the pump gallery to prevent the rotor fouling.

The rapid bearing wear results largely from the extra weight of the pistons and, again, the longer stroke. These impose rather heavy stresses on the crankshaft: that component resists wear because it is nitrided and the bearing shells suffer instead.

One minor fault which can be most annoying is that the plastic rotor arm has a habit of shearing off at the distributor shaft at high revs. This is thought to be due to a vibration frequency peculiar to this engine. Special competition rotors with metal inserts are available and have largely overcome this problem.

A point often missed is that the 1275 engine is rather heavier than the smaller-capacity units, something which may have to be taken into account in relation to suspension modifications.

A trouble experienced from time to time when racing the S engine and subjecting it continually to 8,000rpm-plus is that the small restrictors in the crankshaft oilways are thrown out, causing loss of oil pressure and resulting overheating of the pistons and little ends, which can be most unpleasant. I know of no remedy for this, and one just has to trust to luck or carry out frequent inspections.

Cylinder head
With the exception of the amount to be machined off the head face to obtain the compression ratio required, all modifications are identical, whether the engine be a 970, 1071 or 1275. In general, I refer only to the 'blue' head, since I would use no other, though the 'yellow' head can be treated similarly. As will be seen from the diagram, the combustion chambers and ports of the Cooper S head are different in shape to those found on other A-series engines. Much less metal needs to be removed to get close to the ideal shape, though the basic principles remain the same.

As before, the inlet tracts are a main focus of attention. The ports should be lightly polished, and maybe even slightly enlarged, and the valve throats should be thoroughly smoothed. In much the same manner as described earlier for the other Mini heads, the valve guides and bosses should be reshaped and the seats blended into a single radius.

The valves themselves cannot be enlarged and already have an excellent shape, but slight improvement is still possible along the lines detailed earlier. These valves are longer than those

Modifying the Cooper S combustion chamber. Metal is removed from the shaded areas. Less modification is required than with other Mini cylinder heads. The maker has already provided some relieving around the inlet valve.

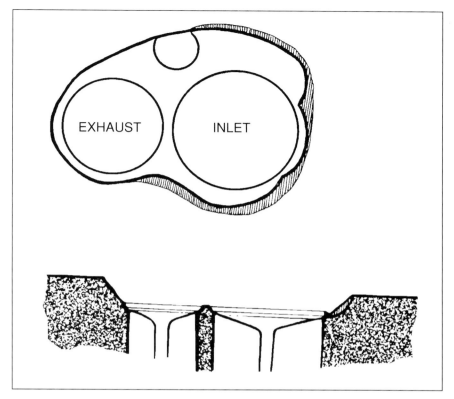

fitted to the ordinary Mini/Cooper/1100 engines to allow for the use of a high-lift full-race camshaft.

When modifying the combustion chambers, care must be taken to ensure that the gasket is not undercut, for not only will this destroy the gasket seal, it will not improve the gas-flow properties of the head. Nevertheless, the sloping chamber walls can be brought nearer the vertical in the areas directly adjacent to the inlet valves and opposite the sparking plugs. The walls should be given a nice smooth radius and, apart from the beak, all projections removed completely.

It will be noticed that there is very little metal between the inlet and exhaust valve (hence the fact that the valves cannot be enlarged) and because of the position of the valve seats the division between the valves is in fact a sharp-edged ridge. This ridge gets hot, probably white hot under competition conditions, and subsequent rapid cooling can cause the metal to crack between the valve seats. This cracking is quite common on the Cooper S and constitutes a serious problem. With this in mind, the sharp edge should be removed, and the division can usefully be blended into the inlet valve seat radius, but great care must be taken not to reduce the width of the exhaust valve

seat by more than a few thousandths of an inch. By removing the sharp edge and creating a smooth radius, one minimizes the possibilities for very localized overheating at this spot, hence the metal is not subjected to such extreme temperature variations and the tendency to crack is lessened. I am not claiming that this is the complete answer, and I can't prove that it specifically eliminates the problem, but I do know that all the Cooper S heads that I have been associated with have been modified in this way and none of them has cracked.

Camshafts
For racing purposes the only worthwhile camshaft available, unless you are in a position to design your own, is the manufacturer's 648 type, previously called 649. This cam has the incidental advantage that the standard S distributor needs no modification for its use as the characteristics of the two are already matched. Neither is it necessary to fit longer valves or modify the valve spring seats because, as already mentioned, this engine is designed to accommodate a high-lift camshaft, having been developed with racing in mind. It is necessary, however, to fit special long

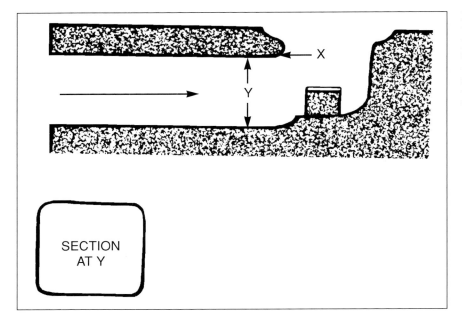

SECTION
AT Y

Diagrammatic section through Cooper S inlet port. Note much thinner section of metal at X compared with other A-series heads, also small valve guide boss and 'square' port section.

tappet adjusting screws, BMC part number C-AEA 692. They should be set to give 0.015in (15 thou) clearance. As an alternative to fitting the longer tappet adjusters, it is possible simply to machine 0.050in (50 thou) off the base of each rocker shaft pedestal.

For road use there are effectively three alternatives: the standard Cooper camshaft, type 948 (yes, it is more vigorous than the standard Cooper S component, which is AEA 630), the 731 or the 544. I have never tried the latter in a Cooper S, but I should think it would make an excellent high-performance road-cum-sprint cam if its characteristics in other A-series engines are anything to go by. My experience with the 948 and 731 camshafts has shown them both to provide excellent torque and much improved top-end power, while still giving good fuel economy. (The 648 racing cam can plunge petrol consumption to something like 10 to 12mpg!)

Special camshafts are of course available from a number of the tuning shops, and some of them are the result of serious development work. The reputation and results of the firm concerned will be some guide. But often they are very similar to the BMC products anyway, making any extra cost difficult to justify. I do know of one case where someone purchased a special high-performance camshaft for an ordinary Sprite, and paid a very high specialist price for it: close inspection revealed a standard 948 camshaft, which is just what BMC themselves suggest at far lower cost.

Carburettors and manifolds

Standard equipment is identical to that of the ordinary Cooper except that the S inlet manifold is fitted with a union for the vacuum brake servo connection. Probably the commonest carburettors used on modified engines are twin 1½in SU H4s, on a standard or specialist-manufactured manifold, and set up as already described for other Mini models. The needles and piston springs used will of course depend upon the individual engine and the camshaft fitted. With a hot camshaft like the 648/649, a good starting point for needles would be CP4 for the 970 engine, MME for the 1071 and BG for the 1275, with blue piston springs for the two smaller units, red for the larger.

A single 45 DCOE Weber carburettor is favoured by many competition enthusiasts, though once again opinion is varied about the extent of the advantage over twin SUs and it is not always easy to sort out the facts from the mythology. But the general consensus seems to be favourable. Unfortunately I have no experience of this carburettor and so I can give no advice other than to say that most of the tuning specialists who sell them should be able to advise what jets should be used. If using this carburettor, it will be found necessary to alter the position of the wiring loom near the speedometer and also to cut away the bulkhead slightly in the same area.

I have seen several set-ups which involve the use of twin 38 DCOE Webers, but frankly I fail to see what possible advantages there can be in feeding one siamesed inlet port with two carburettor chokes. However, everyone to their own theories! To me, it would seem just to make the tuning procedure far more complicated, which may well ultimately result in less power when compared with a simpler arrangement – and that's without raising the question of cost.

One final word on carburettors. Although they are still not commonly fitted, downdraught racing Weber carburettors are claimed by people using them to provide gains of up to 7 or 8bhp, and from what I have seen these claims would appear to be justified. Unfortunately, I understand that these carbs are also exceedingly difficult to tune accurately, and I know of several cases where this has brought about a reversion to the sidedraught 45 DCOE or twin SUs. Also, one big disadvantage for many people is that the cost is very high, and clearly rolling-road tuning or some other kind of professional help is likely to have to be added on top of the initial outlay to get the best out of the set-up. A modified bonnet will be needed too.

With almost any carburettor arrangement, useful gains in some parts of the rev range may be made by varying the length of the induction manifold, in conjunction with changes to the length and conformation of the exhaust system, but it is very difficult to give precise instructions as the final layout is very much a matter of experiment and depends upon a large number of variable factors.

For road use, the standard exhaust manifold should prove entirely adequate, though for competition purposes long-branch manifolds can be obtained and give good results when used in conjunction with the 648/649 camshaft. These manifolds are part number C-AEG 432 for the 970 and 1071 and C-AEG 365 for the 1275 engine. Some tuning specialists sell their own designs, but they tend to be very similar.

Other engine modifications

If rebuilding an S engine, note that the connecting rods on the 970 version are of a different length from those fitted to the 1071 or 1275. The block may be bored a maximum of +0.040in (40 thou), but with the 1275 engine this results in a capacity in excess of 1,300cc which may prove an embarrassment if participation in any competition with a class division at that size is envisaged. It should be noted that if the engine is bored to that maximum dimension the tops of

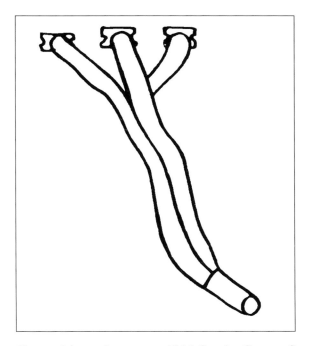

Competition exhaust manifold for the Cooper S engine has very long separate branches for optimum flow with a racing camshaft.

the bores must not be chamfered as that would expose the gasket and may cause it to burn out.

Elsewhere in this book I have referred to the use of flat-topped pistons as being a useful tuning aid. In fact that is only part of the story: concave, dished pistons come nearer to the ideal spherical combustion space, but in many cases it is necessary to depart from this ideal to obtain a high enough compression ratio, which is of greater importance. Thus on an ordinary A-series engine (850, 998 etc) developed for racing, pistons will probably of necessity be flat-topped, or only very slightly dished, in order to achieve a compression ratio in the region of 12:1. The exact shape depends on just how much it is practical to reduce the volume of the combustion chambers in the head. On the 1275 Cooper S, though, it is now common practice to use well dished standard pistons, better results often being obtained that way than with the optional flat-topped pistons.

For related reasons, the shallowness of the combustion chambers precludes the use of projecting-nose sparking plugs on the smaller-capacity engines, as there is a danger that they will foul the piston crown at top dead centre. Again, the situation is different with the 1275 S, and projecting-nose plugs such as Champion

N60Y are often used in this engine for racing.

For competition, and racing in particular, where ultimate horsepower figures are all-important, some people habitually use in excess of 9,000rpm and I know of one who claims to use 10,000rpm on the 970 engine. Those are very high speeds for an engine with pushrod-operated valves, and they demand that the valve gear be so extensively lightened that it would make the standard components in almost any ferrous metal too weak. Thus other materials become necessary, and some people have used rockers, pushrods, spring collars and collets machined from titanium. As you can well imagine, this is a most expensive procedure, always supposing the titanium is available in the first place.

Less extreme measures have been catered for by BMC's own tuning parts operation. These include front pulleys of different sizes, designed to slow down the dynamo and water pump, for with competitors using up to 9,000rpm, especially with the 970, it was found that these parts were being taken beyond their stress limits and suffering damage. These pulleys of course involve the use of a fan belt of different length. Special high-capacity oil and water radiators are available for racing engines, and are essential for the 1275, as also is the export-specification fan.

The manufacturers' tuning manual, listing all the parts available for modifying the Cooper S (and other Minis), is an invaluable guide to what BMC have found necessary, and has regularly been amended by updated information sheets and pamphlets. But certain expenses can be avoided by do-it-yourself techniques, such as lightening your own valve gear rather than buying lightened rockers ready made.

When using a racing camshaft such as the 648/649, the loadings on the valve gear, and the cam followers in particular, are tremendous, and the same is true of bearing loads when engine speeds of 8,000rpm or more are used regularly. In my experience the only lubricants which are fully effective in standing up to these conditions are the castor-based oils such as Castrol R.

Other engine modifications follow the same lines as for the lesser Mini power units. This section has laid a lot of emphasis on very high revs and racing conditions, and it is perhaps worth a reminder that as a road-car engine the 1275 has the great virtue that it is torquey enough not to need to be screamed up to astronomical rpm to obtain very satisfactory performance. A little tuning work, adding the refinement that

mass production cannot afford, can help to realize its potential without enormous cost.

Transmission
The standard gear ratios are similar to those fitted to the Cooper and are quite suitable for ordinary road use. For competition purposes, however, optional close-ratio gears are available in either helical or straight-cut form. While the former are generally adequate for the 970 and 1071 models, it is not unknown for a well tuned 1275 to develop enough torque to strip the helical intermediate gears. It was this which led several specialists and later BMC themselves to produce gears with straight-cut teeth which, though noisy (very noisy!), are far stronger. Since the introduction of these for competition cars, no further trouble has been experienced and, properly assembled, this is a really delightful gearbox. The advantage of using the BMC gears is that they are much cheaper than most of the specialist-manufactured versions.

It is also possible to obtain straight-cut transfer and final drive gears which are specialist-made and hence very expensive. The use of an all-straight-cut transmission does give a small bonus of about 2 or 3bhp in reduced power losses which is worthwhile for racing. Such gears also tend to be much stronger. But they are diabolically noisy as well, and intolerable for road use.

A number of different final-drive ratios are available and the choice will depend on the use to which the vehicle is to be put, the venue for competition in the case of a racing or sprinting machine, and to some extent the state of tune of the engine. A good general ratio for the 1275 is the 3.94:1, while a numerically lower ratio giving higher overall gearing may be useful at some circuits. For the 1071 or 970, 3.94:1 is likely to be the highest useful gearing, and the lower overall ratio provided by the 4.1:1 final drive may well be more appropriate.

Remember that although lower gearing theoretically means using higher revs, with the attendant stress and wear, this is only true in practice where top gear is held on a long straight. Gearing that is too high may in fact require more use of high revs in the intermediate gears to bring road speed up to the point where the next gear can be used, and hanging on to the lower gears in that way is more often the cause of engine damage than over-revving in top.

With the advent of the 1275 Cooper S, racing drivers found that, as a result of the extra power

Negative camber at the front wheels can be achieved by lengthening the lower suspension arms. Adding a quarter of an inch to their length gives a nominal 1½ degrees negative camber.

The suspension arms should be reinforced by boxing in the H-section with steel plate as shown. Safety demands the highest standards of workmanship in any such modifications.

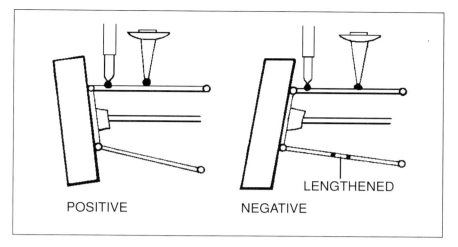

POSITIVE   NEGATIVE   LENGTHENED

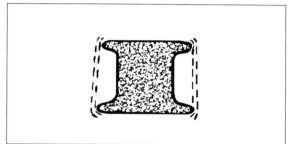

available, wheelspin and violent understeer became a problem. To combat this, a limited-slip differential was produced. This gave fabulous roadholding, greatly reducing the understeer characteristic, and one could throw the S about as easily as an ordinary Cooper or Mini. It did, however, make the car even more prone to handling variations with abrupt changes of power at the front wheels caused by the transition from throttle open to throttle shut or vice versa. This is noticeable even in a straight line and quite a lot of finesse is called for to drive a Cooper S thus equipped in a smooth and non-erratic manner – but then people who can't manage that probably shouldn't race anyway!

Brakes, suspension and wheels

As we have seen already, the Cooper S is fitted with better brakes than any other Mini and they really work. The only really necessary modification for hard use is to fit uprated pads and linings such as Ferodo DS 11 front and VG 95 rear or equivalents. Extra brake cooling by the judicious use of vents in the front valance, in the manner already described for ordinary Minis, is advantageous.

Most people who race the Cooper S find that they prefer to drive with the servo put out of operation by disconnecting it even when regulations forbid its removal. Basically, they find that the servo destroys part of the driver's braking sensitivity and is not capable of reacting as quickly as the ordinary direct hydraulic system.

The standard Cooper S wheels are very strong, and 4½in-wide steel rims are an option obtainable quite cheaply. Many racing Minis, however, can be seen fitted with magnesium alloy or aluminium alloy wheels in an effort to reduce unsprung weight. I would say that any advantages of this kind were very marginal in their effect on roadholding, and I would only bother to fit such wheels on the front, the biggest influence then being on the steering. Similarly, any benefits in terms of reduced overall weight and improved brake cooling are very hard to quantify.

But if a limited-slip differential is fitted then those lightweight wheels at the front assume a most important role. The strain on the drive-shafts and universal joints is very much increased by the modified diff, and the heavier the road wheels are the greater that strain becomes, because of their greater inertia. Any reduction in wheel weight reduces the inertia and the consequent loads on the shafts. It has been found that simply replacing standard steel 4½in front wheels with magnesium alloy ones halves the rate of wear on the universal joints under racing conditions!

There is very little point in trying to increase further the track of the Cooper S by using extra spacers as it is already wider than an ordinary Mini: if a vehicle becomes too wide in relation to its length it becomes very difficult to handle and decidedly twitchy, especially in the wet, apart from

Starting point: this is a pristine, unmodified Mk2 Austin Mini-Cooper S 1275. The appearance was very close to that of an ordinary Mini, making it a super little Q-car.

the risk of overloading wheel studs and bearings.

Earlier in the book I have mentioned giving the wheels negative camber and altering the front castor angle. These are beneficial but subtle modifications and easily over-done. The degree of change is a matter of individual choice and preferences in handling characteristics, so I am going to outline the method without prescribing the amount.

Alterations to the castor angle are made by altering the length of the tie-bars linking the hubs to the front of the subframe. One can either buy or make up adjustable tie-bars, which is ideal, or merely alter the length of the existing components by fitting rubber spacers of different thickness. It is possible to cut the tie-bar and fit a sleeve over the cut, but very strong welding is essential – I would personally not use this technique because of the dangers involved.

The front wheels can be set to a negative camber angle by two methods. The first is to move the drillings in the front subframe, where the transverse suspension arms are bolted, further out from the vehicle centre. I have no experience of doing this, and caution would prompt me to weld on some ³⁄₁₆in steel plates as reinforcement, because this operation moves the holes very close to the edge of the subframe and the arm could feasibly tear away at this point. The second, simpler and quite safe method involves lengthening the lower suspension arm. It can either be heated and stretched or cut and rewelded with an insert to give extra length. In either case the arm should be additionally strengthened by welding ³⁄₁₆in steel

plate along the sides to box in the H-section. Properly done, this results in a stronger than standard component. But if you have any doubt about your own ability to carry out these suspension modifications, either leave well alone or get some expert help – the possible consequences of suspension breakage are deterrent enough.

Rear wheel negative camber is most easily and reliably obtained by altering the drillings in the rear subframe where the swinging arm is bolted on. The drilling nearest the vehicle centre should be moved closer to ground level while the outer drilling should be moved upwards. In fact it is quite safe just to alter the outer drilling and bend the inner subframe to suit.

All other suspension modifications are as for ordinary Minis. One other change which does not strictly affect the suspension does become necessary when the vehicle is lowered and wider wheels or spacers are employed, especially if racing is envisaged, and this too applies to all Minis. The outer part of the rear wheelarches should be cut away from the body panel, raised further into the body, slightly reprofiled and then rewelded. Otherwise the rear tyres will rub when cornering hard; this is particularly likely with wide racing tyres. Unfortunately this is quite a tricky operation, and unless you are possessed of considerable ability and experience in this kind of metalwork, it is cheaper and more satisfactory in the long run to leave it to a professional. Also, when using wide tyres, it will be found necessary to cut the upper dust shroud off the rear shock absorber to prevent fouling.

12

Non-S 1275 engines

The first A-series power unit of 1,275cc capacity was the largest of three Mini-Cooper S versions, with the special, sport-orientated features we have already discussed. Later came a more normal production version, in two basic forms. There is a longitudinally-mounted type as fitted to Mk4 Sprites and Mk3 Midgets, and a transverse type fitted first to 1300 versions of what had been the Austin/Morris 1100 and then to the Mini Clubman GT.

Both types are basically similar, but the Sprite/Midget cylinder head is retained by nine studs while the transverse type has eleven. The Spridgets, the 1300 GT saloon and the cars wearing Riley and Wolseley disguise have twin 1¼in SU carburettors, while the non-GT 1300 saloons and the 1275 Mini Clubman have single carburettors.

There is inevitably some confusion among enthusiasts about the exact differences between these engines and the Cooper S unit, and about their relative advantages and disadvantages. When the 1,275cc engine first appeared for the sports cars, most people assumed that it was just a Cooper S unit slightly modified for its new lengthways accommodation. But the knowledgeable soon spotted that there were only nine head studs as compared to eleven on the S. That is not all, however, variations from the S specification being more than just superficial.

Perhaps of most interest, because of its applicability to other engines, is the cylinder head. Though the port and chamber shapes in the head are similar, valve sizes are not. Both inlet and exhaust are smaller and, although the exhaust valves are made in Nimonic, the inlet valves are not of such high-quality material as those in the S head. But, like the S head, this one is free of the oilway running just below the face, as found in other A-series heads, so the problem of breaking into the oilway when machining to raise the compression ratio is once again absent.

With experience, tuners have come to recognize that this Mk4 head, as it has become known, is a useful source of extra power on any racing Mini, whether it be an 850 or a full-house 1,293cc Cooper S. The important point is that while it is not possible to increase the valve sizes in the Cooper S head, this head, provided the exhaust valves remain standard size, can accommodate even larger inlet valves than the S. Thus on Cooper S-derived racers we find inlet valves up to ¹⁄₁₆in larger than S specification. Even on 1,293cc racers, the smaller exhaust valve has proven adequate though not in itself beneficial. On 850 and 998 Mini racers, the smaller exhaust valve of the Mk4 head compared with the S is a distinct advantage (valves can be too large, as we have seen, slowing rather than assisting gas flow) while the inlet valves can go up to standard S size. This is larger than can be fitted to any of the more ordinary heads such as the 12G 295 (998 Cooper and MG 1100) casting. For these reasons the Mk4 head has emerged as the superior head for all racing applications.

Both nine and eleven-stud versions can be considered as Mk4 heads, but it is of course necessary to drill the two extra holes in the former to convert it for use on a Cooper S or 1300 GT block. One potential problem with the Mk4 head has already been touched on earlier in the book: from the valve seat to the bottom of the valve spring locating groove, it is thicker than any of the other A-series heads, which means that the valves are longer. If other valves are fitted, Cooper S ones for example, standard-length valve springs are too long and spring crush can result. Suitable valves, in standard Mk4 and Cooper S sizes later became available from BL Special Tuning, but before that some people had special valves made at considerable cost. Somewhat cheaper was the solution I adopted when fitting Cooper S valves to a Mk4 head, which was to use extra-strong Cortina 1500 GT springs. The Mk4 head is fitted with standard iron valve guides and for high-revving use these should be replaced with Hidural bronze-alloy ones from one of the specialist suppliers such as Janspeed.

Because the Mk4 head was designed for an engine with the same bore centres as found on the Cooper S, it can only be used as an outright racing tweak on the more mundane A-series units, on which the bore centres are different. If you put the head on, say, an 850 block, this difference in cylinder spacing results in a reduction in squish area and consequent bad effects on turbulence and combustion characteristics which can only be overcome by bumping the compression ratio up in the region of 13:1, a figure not acceptable on other than a racing engine. The problem does not, of course arise on a 1,275cc unit, S or otherwise.

The cylinder block of the non-S 1,275cc engine lacks the inspection plates over the cam-follower chest which other units have, being solid in this region. This is allegedly to increase rigidity, though I am inclined to think that it is more likely to be a cost-cutting measure. It certainly makes it damned difficult to work on that part of the valve gear.

Real increases in rigidity are to be found around the main-bearing housings and the flange which bolts to the gearbox casing. The housings are much stronger and stiffer and the flange is more than twice as thick as on the S unit. Some other, later A-series engines have this thicker flange as well. It was an effort to prevent movement of the block relative to the gearbox casing and the resultant gasket failures and oil leaks. Unfortunately, there is some evidence that it has given rise to localized stresses: instead of flexing evenly as the 1275 S block does under racing conditions this later block sometimes cracks around the dipstick hole.

One authority maintains that this is because people lighten the flywheel too much and thereby lose its damping effect on torsional vibrations. While I agree that flywheels can be over-lightened, it is strange that the same degree of lightening causes no problems with the S block.

The connecting rods for this engine are somewhat similar to the S pattern but much heavier, with large counterbalance weights on the big-end caps in an effort to overcome the roughness which seems to be characteristic of the 1300 unit when it is in standard trim and has not been balanced. The standard crankshaft is Tuftrided rather than nitrided as on the original S. But I understand that in the interests of economy many later S crankshafts are also Tuftrided, and in this case S and 1300 cranks would be identical, with only the necessary variation at the flywheel end of the longitudinally-mounted version. To give a lower compression ratio, 1300 pistons are much more dished than the Cooper S pattern. There are variations, too, in the type of oil-pump drive and consequently the tail of the camshaft, more details of which can be found in Chapter 17.

Beyond these differences, the 1300 and Cooper S units can in practical terms be considered as pretty well identical. Do remember, though, if you are tempted to fit a 1275 Cooper S block to a Sprite or a Midget or even a Morris 1000, that it will be necessary to make a complete new rear main-bearing cap, as those on the lengthways engine differ in shape from those on the transverse version.

13

Carburettors

The number and variety of carburettors which have been offered on the market as tuning aids for the Mini are legion and some are much more successful than others, particularly if effectiveness is weighed against cost. This chapter looks at two specific carburettors, the 1½in SU H4 and the 1½in Reece-Fish. The reason for choosing these two is that they emerged as the most popular instruments to use in the Mini 7 saloon racing formula, the regulations for which restricted carburation to a single unit with a maximum choke tube diameter of 1½in. The SU was inexpensive, readily available second-hand, simple, and gave excellent results when properly set up. The Reece-Fish was its only real challenger and became recognized as the complete answer to carburation for the formula because it offered a bonus in power and performance yet was also very simple and in many respects easier to tune than an SU.

The SU H4 carburettor

Why do I suggest using the H4 version of the SU rather than the 1½in HS4 which was a later design? Well, the flange which fixes it to the manifold is nearer to being universal: it has the same attachment stud spacing as a standard Mini HS2 carb. Should you wish to use a standard manifold for cost reasons, second-hand manifolds to suit this carb are more plentiful. The manifold fixings are also the same as those of the Reece-Fish, so that you can change from one to the other without the extra cost of another manifold. The

H4 has a slightly longer choke tube than the HS4 and it is my opinion that this aids gas flow through the carburettor by increasing gas velocity, ram-tube fashion. This may be only marginal, but even margins are important when racing.

Before trying to sort the mixture setting, you must first get the carb set up properly, with all the necessary modifications complete. If you assemble an SU carburettor and raise the piston as far as you can with your finger, you will usually find that even at full lift, as far away from the bridge across the lower part of the choke tube as it will go, the piston still partially projects into the choke tube, thus effectively reducing its diameter and gas-flow capacity. The reason is that quite often the damper tube, which is part of the piston, is too long, and at full lift it fouls the screw cap on top of the piston cover, preventing the piston rising any further. The remedy is unsubtle but simple: shorten the tube on top of the piston by sawing or grinding an appropriate amount off the top. Remember that you must clean up the resultant cut edge, removing any burrs, as these will otherwise prevent the piston sliding up and down freely, which would be disastrous to performance.

Next, modify the piston itself. To begin with, it should be of the quick-lift variety, which used to be obtainable direct from SU or from tuning specialists: more recently, the supply seems to have dried up, but no doubt if you went along to your local engine tuners armed with your standard piston they would do the job for you

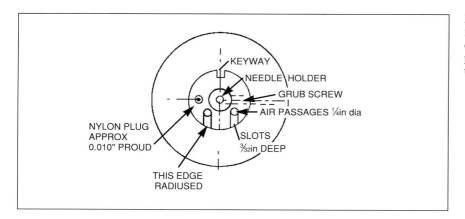

Modifying the SU piston for quick lift involves drilling two new air passages in the underside.

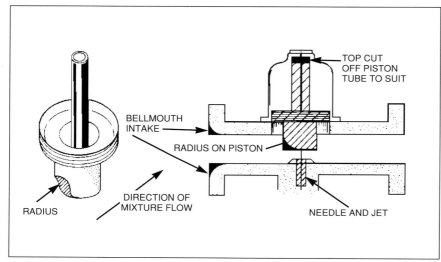

Other SU carburettor modifications include radiusing the leading edge of the piston and trimming the top of the piston damper tube if necessary to ensure that full lift is possible.

quite cheaply. If you have trouble, try Janspeed in Salisbury.

Alternatively, it is possible to do the job yourself. The existing hole in the side of the piston should be blanked off and two new holes of ¼in diameter, with slots ³⁄₃₂in deep, made in the underside of the piston as shown in the diagram.

The lower leading edge of the piston, that is the edge away from the manifold and towards the air intake, should be smoothly radiused off for about three-eighths of its circumference, the greatest radius (about ⅜in) being in line with the longitudinal centre line of the choke tube, and tapering off to nothing either side, stopping opposite the bridge. No attempt should be made to radius the manifold side of the piston, or the bridge. The air intake mouth of the carburettor can also be rounded off, unless some additional intake pipe or trumpet is to be fitted. Ordinary hand tools can be used for these operations (with

care: the alloy of which the carburettor is made is relatively soft and easily damaged) and a final polish obtained with wet-and-dry emery paper.

The butterfly can have its leading edge – towards the air intake – knife edged (but without reducing its overall diameter which would in effect prevent the throttle from being closed completely), the spindle diameter can be reduced and the butterfly fixing screws should be cut off flush with the spindle, all in the interests of reducing obstructions to airflow through the carburettor.

It is also possible to modify the linkage so that the butterfly opens the other way round. That is, instead of the bottom half of the butterfly moving towards the air intake and the top half towards the manifold, you make it vice versa: this will give slightly better throttle response.

Most people find that a full-race 850 Mini fitted with the 649 camshaft and large-valve head requires a very rich mixture. Even the SU 0.090

needle, type BG, is too weak. All you can do is make the needle slightly thinner over the bottom quarter of its length, where it is already thinnest, to richen the mixture at higher revs. I can't tell you how much: the full-race engine is very susceptible to even small changes in engine and exhaust system specification. It is necessary to experiment and arrive at the right answer by trial and error, using plug tests as a guide.

You will probably find that if you stick to the recommended fuel level in the float chamber, the car will be almost undrivable in right-hand corners, at least at racing speeds – the engine will cut dead. Most unpleasant, and potentially very dangerous! There are three ways of overcoming this. I found that the simplest way was quite effective. The float control arm was bent up so that it touched the float chamber lid and the needle valve never closed. Consequently, if the ignition was switched on but the engine not started, the whole lot flooded. If the car was left parked facing downhill, petrol siphoned out of the tank straight through the float chamber on to the ground. All, of course, quite unacceptable for a road car! But this was an out-and-out racer, the side effects were tolerable in my opinion – they disappeared when the engine was running – and I overcame my fuel surge problem.

The second answer is to fit an additional float chamber, so that you have one either side of the main carburettor body. The additional bowl is simple enough to fit, using a long fixing bolt double-drilled with two fuel feed holes. Unfortunately you will find the throttle linkage a real nuisance to arrange. Being lazy, I did not use this method, even though I had the necessary bits.

A third solution takes the form of a special, extended float chamber lid which SU themselves produced. This increases the overall height of the float chamber, enabling the float to be set at a much higher level. If you can get one, this is probably the best remedy for the age-old surge problem and it is very easy to fit, being a straight substitute for the standard component.

(Longer term, the answer to a variety of fuel-level problems arrived at by SU was the HIF type carburettor, with its annular float chamber surrounding the jet assembly. That carburettor, though, had a number of other differences, including a swing needle mounting, which put it beyond the scope of the current discussion.)

So there it is, a simple, effective, cheap carburettor. Yes, the Reece-Fish proved better from a power standpoint: but don't let that put you off competing if you can't afford something more exotic than the SU. You can still go very quickly on an SU, and have a lot of fun – and the knowledge that you still have a fair bit of development left is always most comforting.

The Reece-Fish carburettor
The 1½in Reece-Fish came to be regarded by most people, myself included, as the ultimate in carburation on a formula Mini 7 racing saloon. But the fact that I am considering this carburettor in the light of Mini racing experience does not at all mean that this is its sole application: it has proved most effective on a wide range of road and rally production cars, whether or not the engine is otherwise modified. This is one major difference between the SU H4 and the Reece-Fish: the SU only really gives better results – when compared with an original-equipment carburettor – on the BMC A-series engine, and then only with capacities up to 1,100cc. Thus its use, in single form, as a tuning extra is rather limited. No one in their right mind, for example, would think of fitting a single SU H4 in place of the standard Weber on a Cortina GT. But the 1½in Reece-Fish gives excellent results on almost any engine up to 2 litres, including the Cortina, where it is used to replace single-choke or progressive twin-choke set-ups. It is far more universal and, used singly, has often given better results than twin carburettors or multiple choke instruments, particularly where siamesed inlet ports are used.

The Reece-Fish comes in several forms, including a downdraught version used to replace other downdraught carburettors and a semi-downdraught used, as in the Mini application, to replace carburettors like the SU or Zenith-Stromberg on inclined manifolds. Two sizes, 1½in and 1¼in have also been produced. Tuning procedures and the method of operation, though, are identical for all types, and I am indebted to the makers' own literature for much of what follows.

Apart from having a float feed, the Reece-Fish carburettor is entirely different from other types as it has no choke tube, taper needle, jets or air strangler. The fuel level is relatively unimportant and the only moving parts are the throttle spindle, needle valve and leaf valve. The float chamber is comprised of two compartments separated by a metal diaphragm which carries a leaf valve – one containing the float, while the other houses the radial fuel pick-up arm attached to the throttle spindle. The fuel is metered for the relative throttle openings by a horizontal hole in

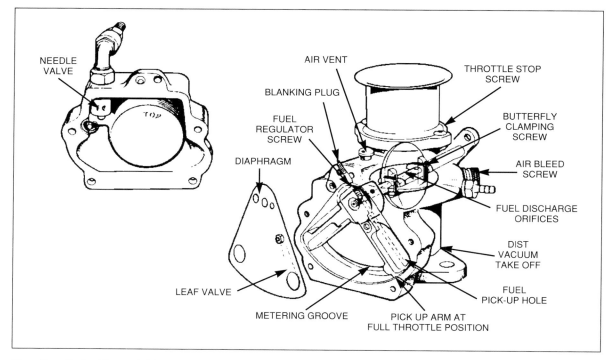

NEEDLE VALVE

AIR VENT

THROTTLE STOP SCREW

BLANKING PLUG

BUTTERFLY CLAMPING SCREW

FUEL REGULATOR SCREW

AIR BLEED SCREW

DIAPHRAGM

FUEL DISCHARGE ORIFICES

DIST VACUUM TAKE OFF

FUEL PICK-UP HOLE

LEAF VALVE

METERING GROOVE

PICK UP ARM AT FULL THROTTLE POSITION

Details of the Reece-Fish carburettor, a brilliantly simple design. It is unfortunately no longer in production, but second-hand examples are available from time to time.

the pick-up arm which registers with a calibrated groove machined radially in the chamber wall, passes through the pick-up arm, and is discharged through the orifices in the throttle spindle. As the pick-up arm fits closely into the inner chamber, it also acts as a displacer or piston: when the throttle is opened sharply, the leaf valve closes and the chamber becomes pressurized, forcing fuel through the arm and spindle into the air stream for an acceleration shot.

The carburettor should be fitted with the float chamber facing the front of the car. For this reason, on a lengthways engine, where an inclined or horizontal carburettor is being replaced, a left or right-hand model must be used as appropriate, but this does not apply with a transverse engine. In order to eliminate the risk of heavy loading and consequent wear on the main spindle, the throttle control linkage should operate direct and without bias, preferably through a bell crank or telescopic return spring, and no opposing return springs should be used on the throttle arm.

Each carburettor is bench tested and, where possible adjusted to the engine capacity for which it is intended. However, individual tuning is essential after fitment and can be divided into two stages, maximum power setting and cruising range adjustment.

Maximum power is obtained by using the socket key provided and adjusting the fuel flow regulator screw in the pick-up arm with the engine running at full throttle under load. Turn clockwise to weaken and the reverse to enrich until the optimum is reached. As can be seen in the diagram, this screw is only accessible at the full throttle position after the blanking plug has been removed.

This operation should be carried out on a roller dynamometer for the quickest and best results. Alternatively, adjustment can be made on the road by using an uphill section of about half a mile. Approach a roadside marker at 40mph, opening the throttle fully as the marker is passed and noting the speedometer reading at two or more points on the climb. With the engine stopped, the mixture strength should now be weakened by turning the regulator screw clockwise one flat on the hexagonal key. Replace the blanking plug. Repeat the run under exactly the same conditions, again noting the speedometer readings. If an improvement is shown, weaken the mixture further by the same amount. If there is no improvement, it can be assumed that the mixture is already too weak and must be enriched by turning the regulator screw two flats anti-clockwise – that is one flat beyond the initial setting.

Continue the test runs, adjusting one flat at a time until power is noticed to drop off, then return the regulator screw to the previous best setting. Having attained maximum power, weaken the mixture strength slightly, less than one flat, to ensure maximum economy together with peak performance.

Next, check the cruising range adjustment. For maximum output and peak efficiency from an engine, the ideal air-fuel ratio of 15:1 should remain constant throughout the throttle range. As peak efficiency produces the highest manifold vacuum reading, that reading can be used to check that the air-fuel ratio is correct. By altering the relative radial positions on the spindle of the throttle butterfly controlling the air and the pick-up arm controlling the amount of fuel metered by the groove until the highest vacuum reading is obtained, the correct mixture ratio and peak efficiency will be assured. A good quality vacuum gauge must be used when making the adjustment.

Close the air bleed screw lightly against its seating and then open it half a turn. Remove the plug and connect the vacuum gauge. Start the engine and run it until normal working temperature is attained. Partly loosen the butterfly clamping screw to allow restricted radial movement using the key: the butterfly needs to be movable on the spindle but not loose. Adjust the throttle stop screw to set engine speed to 2,000rpm. Using a suitable scriber, block the centre hole in the butterfly spindle, noting the effect on the vacuum gauge reading.

Vacuum rise indicates weak mixture which can be corrected by closing the butterfly slightly, thereby admitting less air for the same amount of fuel. This can best be effected with a light tap on the upper half of the butterfly using the blunt end of the scriber. Vacuum fall indicates a rich mixture. In this case it is necessary to admit more air by opening the butterfly, tapping the lower half. After either adjustment, reset engine speed to 2,000rpm.

Repeat the operation until blocking the centre hole in the spindle produces no change in vacuum reading. Tighten the butterfly clamping screw. Check the reading again to ensure that the butterfly did not move as the screw was tightened. Adjust the throttle stop screw for correct tick-over

and, if necessary, alter the air bleed screw setting to correct the idling-speed mixture.

When setting the carburettor on a transverse engine, a mirror, held in the left hand and used like a dentist does, is helpful in locating the butterfly clamping screw and the centre hole in the spindle

The cruising range adjustment must always be checked and reset when any alteration is made to the maximum power mixture adjustment. Ignition timing can generally be advanced some five degrees or more beyond the standard setting. Adjustments should be made progressively and tested under similar conditions to those used to check maximum power.

For cold starting, no hard and fast rule can be given as the best technique will vary from engine to engine, but it is usually best effected by sharply depressing the accelerator pedal once or twice to prime the manifold, then releasing the pedal completely and operating the starter. The engine should fire immediately and may be assisted by gentle pumping on the accelerator until even running at a fast tick-over is obtained, which should be held for a few moments before moving off.

When making adjustments, the throttle should always be opened very slowly to avoid flooding the manifold with the 'accelerator pump' effect already explained. If flooding does occur, making starting difficult, slowly open the throttle fully and hold it still in that position while operating the starter.

Cleanliness of the fuel supply is of utmost importance and an additional filter should be fitted wherever possible. In the event of contamination, the carburettor can be cleaned with an air line after removing the float chamber and diaphragm. No attempt should be made to dismantle the carburettor further as no useful purpose will be served. Care must be taken when replacing the diaphragm to check that it settles into the register provided. To ensure freedom from blockages, fuel can be pumped through the spindle into a container after the carburettor has been removed from the engine.

With a racing car in particular, road testing is difficult or impossible and, although you can substitute track testing, I found that by far the simplest and quickest method was to scrounge the use of a local Crypton rolling road. The usual plug test can be used as a final cross-check on mixture.

That is the basic tuning procedure for the Reece-Fish carburettor. The beauty of it is that it

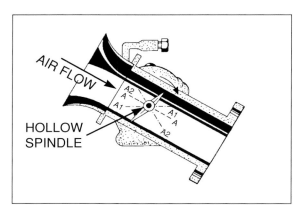

Section of the Reece-Fish choke tube. A, A1, A2 represent different positions of the fuel discharge drillings relative to the butterfly shown fully closed. A–A is a mean position, A1–A1 weakest and A2–A2 richest mixture setting.

allows the instrument to be set accurately for any engine without the need to change jets, needles or other components to achieve the correct calibration. For road cars, and for competition use where the extremes of high engine speeds are not called for, it is perfect. I did run into some problems when using the carburettor for racing, though, and the remedy, once discovered, provided a useful extra technique for the tuner's book of tricks.

For over a year I had no reason to doubt the validity of the method already outlined. After all, these carbs were in everyday use by hundreds of people, and dozens were successfully employed on Mini 7 racers. We had all followed this same tuning procedure and found it completely satisfactory. Certainly, the carburation on my racer, KTR 223E, had been perfect during 1967, the car going like stink as a result.

However, come 1968, KTR had a different engine with an altered cylinder head, necessitating a different mixture setting. Religiously, I followed the standard procedure. At first, all seemed well: I had set the butterfly to give maximum vacuum and was progressively richening the main mixture-control grub screw. Lack of time to hire a circuit for testing and awkward neighbours preventing the use of the rolling road meant that all experiment had to be carried out at actual race meetings, during the very short practice sessions. Each new practice session saw me with a slightly richer mixture setting, using the grub screw, and a little extra power.

Then, at the September Bank Holiday meeting at Lydden Hill, this procedure fell flat on its face.

I had been richening the mixture because it was still far, far too weak at maximum revs and was seriously restricting top-end power. Suddenly it was too rich and, as I put my foot down, the engine went onto three cylinders till revs rose to about 5,000 when it came back onto four. Yet it still wasn't too rich at peak revs, it was too weak: both the exhaust pipe and the plugs were white, and power dropped off badly at 7.000rpm even in second gear.

Don't ask me to explain how you can feel the difference between a misfire due to over-richness and one due to weakness. All I can say is that the former seems to make the engine growl, while the latter causes evident missing with a series of little reports like backfiring: you will know the difference once you have experienced it. Needless to say, I was at first very puzzled. I had followed the accepted sequence which had worked before, but had reached a state of over-richness in the mid range without even approaching a rich enough mixture at peak revs. It was rather like using a carburettor that was too small, but I was convinced that the 1½in Reece-Fish was plenty big enough.

Thinking about it, the butterfly position seemed to dictate the carb's overall setting and determine its general character. The mixture control grub screw merely metered the fuel, the butterfly determined the air-fuel ratio. How could a setting which was perfect at 2,000 or even 3,000rpm be correct at 7,500 to 8,000rpm? It appeared to me that, at very high revs, gas velocity reached a point where, with the relative positions of the butterfly and the spindle drillings, it favoured the air and hindered the petrol flow, weakening the mixture. I figured that though the traditional tuning method was the answer for engines not regularly taken above 7,000rpm, it was not working for higher-revving racers. Even though the mixture-control grub screw was metering enough fuel – in fact too much – into the spindle, the fuel was not in fact escaping through the drillings in sufficient quantities at maximum revs because of the partial masking effect of the butterfly and the pattern of air flow over it.

The obvious answer seemed to me to richen the butterfly setting. But extreme care was needed in this: it was no use relying on the vacuum gauge to indicate the setting, but I still needed to know what setting the butterfly was at, relative to its earlier position. Only that way could I work out an orderly sequence of operations. Then Ken, who looked after the carburettors at the Reece establishment, reminded me that, with the butterfly free to move on the spindle, closing it richens the mixture and opening it weakens the mixture: careful adjustment with the spindle position fixed would enable us to control the degree to which the butterfly was altered from its previous setting without recourse to a vacuum gauge, checking the result by trial and error.

You still need to use a vacuum gauge to obtain a starting point, setting the butterfly for maximum depression, as already described. For really high-revving racers this setting will almost certainly prove too weak, but it is a known point to which you can return if need be. Next take the car out and drive it, or at least rev the engine, taking it up to about 7,000rpm. If it misses, pops, bangs, backfires and generally just won't go, then you know that the grub screw is set too weak. Screw it out till you have eliminated the misfire, exactly as for the earlier maximum power adjustment. Then move on to the following new sequence.

Re-adjust the throttle stop screw by turning it clockwise half a turn, which opens the throttle slightly. Slacken the butterfly clamping screw, push the butterfly to the fully closed position and retighten the clamp. Thus you have now enriched the mixture by an amount which is determined by the alteration you made to the throttle stop screw and hence is defined and repeatable.

This is all the new procedure involves. Unfortunately there is no simple and straightforward sequence whereby you can optimize and forget one setting and then concentrate on the second. With my new method, the grub screw and butterfly settings must be progressively altered together till optimum overall results are obtained. If you reach the point of over-richness on the grub screw, then weaken its setting but continue richening on the butterfly. If the butterfly becomes too rich first, then weaken its setting and richen the grub screw. Keep going until alterations to either only reduce performance. It's time-consuming, very much trial and error, and needs much patience – but anything worthwhile is worth extra effort. Obviously, a dynamometer will make the whole process quicker and more certain.

I have already explained as best I can how to recognize over-rich or weak settings of the grub screw: with the butterfly setting this is easier. If the engine is revved and then the throttle closed, it will momentarily continue to run fast and only slowly return to idle if the setting is too rich. Conversely, if it is too weak, the engine won't start easily. Over richness does not seem to affect top-end performance too badly. In fact, racing engines usually need what would normally be regarded as an over-rich butterfly setting, almost to the point where run-on occurs when shutting the throttle as just described. An engine set up this way does become a little more tempera-mental, difficult to set for idling and prone to foul plugs when fiddling around in the paddock, but perfectly all right once moving on the circuit – a small sacrifice for extra power. I can only assume that somehow that first year I had set the butterfly too rich by accident, getting the right setting by sheer fluke, so that I only needed to adjust the grub screw to obtain optimum racing performance.

One problem encountered on my racing Mini was common to both the SU and Reece-Fish carburettors, and that was fuel surge. Mr Reece came up with the answer in the form of a new wedge-shaped float chamber, wider at the bottom than the top. I still found, however, that I needed to raise the fuel level, by bending the float control arm, to a point where the carburettor flooded if the ignition was left switched on without the engine running for about 45 seconds. With the earlier, more rectangular float chamber, it is necessary to raise the fuel level even higher by grinding or filing a small recess into the chamber top to allow the float to rise higher than would normally be possible. Do not, though, allow this carburettor to flood as much as you might an SU: the needle valve must be capable of working at all times.

No other modification to the Reece-Fish carburettor is required. Its gas-flow characteristics are about as good as they could be, with very little obstruction of the inlet tract – no jet bridge, choke flap or diffuser, just the minimum necessary butterfly and spindle. Very good atomization of the fuel is one of the principal advantages of the design, with a number of small drillings feeding petrol into the centre of the airstream, where gas velocity is highest, rather than a single jet in the venturi wall as in the SU and some other designs. My enthusiasm for this instrument is based on practical experience, and I believe in giving credit where it is due.

14

Using alcohol fuel

It is possible to make an internal combustion engine run on all sorts of different fuels, though petrol and diesel oil have emerged almost unchallenged as the only really practical ones for road vehicles. One alternative which has been used to some extent, though, is alcohol, usually in the form of methanol. It can produce higher power outputs than petrol from an engine of comparable capacity and consequently has been used with some success, when and where the regulations have permitted, in motor sport.

Alcohol is mixed with air and burnt in the engine in much the same way as petrol, but there are some significant differences. The first thing to realize is that when using alcohol fuel the amount by volume that needs to be burnt to obtain a given pressure on the top of the piston is greatly increased. With petrol, the correct air-to-fuel ratio is in the region of 15:1, whereas with alcohol the mixture has to be about 8:1. Secondly, the heat released by alcohol when ignited is less than with petrol, which causes a certain amount of difficulty in obtaining an efficient working temperature. Thirdly, one can use a much higher compression ratio to good advantage, the limit being set by the mechanical strength of the engine rather than the anti-knock properties of the fuel. One other detail is that castor-based lubricants are very soluble in alcohol and so cannot be used because they would immediately be washed off the cylinder walls and piston rings, leading to scuffing, seizure and breakage.

The greatly increased consumption of alcohol fuel compared with petrol, as well as problems with fumes and supply difficulties, render it an impractical fuel for a road-going car (at least while petrol is available). In the UK, and many other countries, there is also the more positive, though artificial, obstacle that it is illegal to use a fuel on which excise duty is not collected, as it is automatically with petrol sales. While those limitations do not necessarily apply in motor sport, the use of alcohol has in practice been very restricted, at least in postwar years, and it is currently banned in all but one or two specific categories which include hillclimbing and sprinting.

That's where the idea of using alcohol in a Mini comes in. Although the contents of this chapter refer to a race-tuned 1,293cc Austin Cooper S, the basic principles involved and the problems encountered would be much the same for almost any other production-based motor car. And although modifying the car to run on alcohol was a rather specialized project, it did throw light on the whole question of matching fuel supply and carburation to the engine, in ways which help in understanding the more normal, petrol-fuelled set-up. The first thing was to decide precisely what fuel to use and, after some consultation, we finally settled on a blend of 90% alcohol, 5% acetone and 5% petrol; then we had to find a supplier. After telephoning various fuel companies with little success, we were eventually put in touch with a supplier in Croydon and a stock of fuel was obtained.

Turning next to lubricant, we were fortunate in being able to obtain a supply of Esso Grand Prix synthetic oil, exactly as used by Jim Clark that year in his World Championship-winning Lotus-Climax. As the car had been running on Castrol R, we were forced to strip the engine and gearbox completely, wash all the parts thoroughly in meths and surgical spirit and then re-assemble them using the Esso oil. That was essential to ensure that no traces of the castor-based oil were left as they would have reacted with the new synthetic lubricant to produce sludge and cause blocked oilways, with obvious dire consequences.

We decided that a 14:1 compression ratio was about as high as the engine would stand without breaking pistons and continually running big-end bearings. A new cylinder head was obtained and gas-flowed much as before, but attention was paid to achieving a high polish to reflect as much heat as possible, so reducing the amount absorbed by the head and helping to offset the problem of low working temperatures already mentioned. For the same reason, we also removed the fan and blanked off the front grille, leaving only an air intake sufficient to feed the carburettors, the net result being a working temperature much the same as had been reached with petrol. That took care of the simplest modifications, the camshaft, pistons, manifolds and type of carburettors (twin 1½in H4 SU) remaining exactly as before.

But the major and most time-consuming operation still remained, which was obtaining the right mixture and the necessary fuel flow. The 8:1 air-fuel ratio with alcohol meant that the flow rate had to be increased by as much as 150 to 200% if starvation and weak mixture were to be avoided. Conversely, an over-rich mixture could quickly cause oil dilution and consequent damage to the engine.

Several days were spent over pints of beer and cups of coffee deciding how best to approach the problem while avoiding too much expense and too much completely new development work, which using a different type of carburettor, for example, would entail. Finally, we reached the following conclusions. Our fuel system needed to be capable of pumping 30 gallons per hour into the inlet manifold, if the carburettor needles were removed. That would give us the required increase in flow, and we would rely solely on the needles for the correct metering under working conditions. We decided to start at the fuel tank and work right through the system step by step, tackling the carburettors and needles last.

Tank capacity was considered first. Fuel consumption on petrol had been about 11mpg, giving a range of 50 to 55 miles on our existing tank. We calculated that consumption would be about 3mpg on alcohol (that was miles out, as will be seen later), giving a range of 15 miles. Since our objective was to compete in the Brighton Speed Trials, run over a standing-start kilometre along Madeira Drive, we felt that our existing tank would be big enough and that, at least, proved to be correct. As much more fuel was to be taken out of the tank per minute, more air obviously had to go in to take its place, so the filler cap had a ⅛in-diameter hole bored in it as a vent.

The existing competition Cooper pattern electric fuel pump, manufactured by SU, was tested and found to deliver about 12 gallons an hour to the carburettors. That was insufficient: we wanted nearer 30 gallons per hour, but without raising supply pressure to a point where the float chamber needle valve was unable to seal and carburettor flooding resulted. We approached SU who were able to provide a double pump which met our requirements.

Tank and pump capacity were now sufficient, but we felt that the internal diameter of the standard fuel line might restrict the flow rate to something below the full output of the pump. This problem was overcome by replacing the line with ⁷⁄₁₆in-bore alcohol-resistant plastic tubing, rerouted inside the car rather than underneath. On testing, we found that the flow rate was now about 30 gallons an hour with little pressure increase. That left the carburettors, in many ways the most difficult job.

Further calculations suggested that we should increase the jet size from 0.090in to 0.125in (an eighth of an inch!) and it turned out that the easiest method was to bore the existing jets out to the new size. Great care and extremely accurate work were obviously the order of the day, and fortunately the operation was completed without hitch. Of course it was no use increasing the jet size without also increasing the delivery capacity of the needle valve feeding the float chamber. Series T4 needle valves were suitable modified, with their bore size doubled.

More tests revealed a flow rate of 27 gallons per hour through the carburettor jets, with no needles fitted. The float chamber needle valves did not protest and no flooding occurred. So the fuel was very effectively being pushed through the carburettors, but now we had to meter it accurately to the engine's requirements. Remember that, in

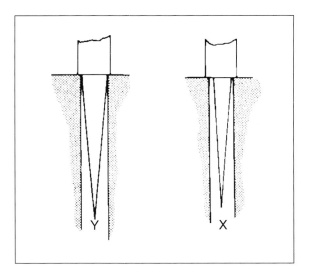

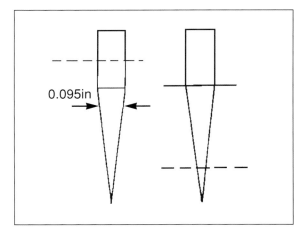

Needles fully inserted in a 0.125in jet, in the piston down, engine stopped position. The 0.090in needle, X, leaves a large gap even in this position, letting too much fuel through and causing an over-rich mixture at low revs. The correct 0.125in needle, Y, almost closes the jet, restricting fuel flow at low revs.

As SU needles of sufficient diameter for our enlarged jets were too long, we tried two methods of shortening them. The wrong way, left, was to cut the needle at the top, in effect moving it up in the piston: this left a diameter of 0.095in at the point of maximum insertion in the 0.125in jet and gave similar results to using a 0.090in needle. The correct way, right, was to cut the tip so that the full 0.124in diameter of the needle was in the jet when the piston was down.

the SU carburettor, fuel is metered by the needle rising and falling in the jet in response to the depressed air pressure in the dashpot. The thicker the part of the needle that is within the jet, the less is the amount of fuel allowed to enter the airstream into the inlet tract. Thick needles give weak mixture, thin needles give rich mixture. At idle, the needle obstructs the jet almost completely and very little fuel enters the airstream. As the throttle opening increases, more air is drawn into the engine, the vacuum in the dashpot increases and the needle rises so that a thinner part is in the jet and more fuel is supplied. That is why the precise taper of the needle is critical and selecting the right needle an essential part of tuning.

First we had to find out the total travel of the needle within the jet, which we did by inserting a simple depth gauge into the dashpot piston, assuming, rightly or wrongly, that the full lift that the dimensions of the carburettor would allow represented the position at full throttle. We also measured the length of needle projecting from the piston and the distance from the underside of the piston to the jet. This gave us the amount of needle in the jet at full lift and with the engine switched off, so that we were able to see over which section of the needle taper the carburettor operated. All this was done with

the needles as used for petrol, since we assumed that the basic engine characteristics would not be altered but simply accentuated and moved up or down the rpm scale. On these findings we based our next modifications.

The existing needles were clearly far too thin to use in conjunction with the enlarged jets. Even if they had by chance been right at full revs, they would have produced far too rich a mixture at lower speeds. In the standard SU range, 0.125in jets are only fitted to 2in carburettors which have much longer needles, so there was nothing 'off the shelf' to suit our requirements. We decided that it was beyond our resources to make our own special needles from scratch, because specialized and extremely accurate grinding equipment is necessary.

After much thought, we took some standard 0.125in-jet needles and reduced the length to that of our existing needles by cutting off the pointed tips. Then we enlisted the help of a friendly watchmaker who kindly agreed to turn the shortened needles down to our own profiles. We had three sets of needles made up this way, one set to the specification we had calculated would be correct, one set a little weaker and the third set richer, so that we would be able to adjust the mixture in the light of testing.

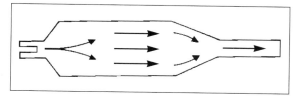

Megaphone 'silencer' fitted to improve exhaust extraction: the resultant increase in gas flow weakened the mixture by just the right amount.

As an interim measure, while these needles were being made, we decided to try another method. Standard 0.125in-jet needles were shortened by cutting them off at the thick end, thus moving them up in the jet. That meant that they were in effect at part-throttle position even at idle, and the result, perhaps predictably, was disastrous. The mixture was much too rich at low revs, fouled the plugs and diluted the oil to the point where it was easily ignited with a match. The most unfortunate side-effect was that the alcohol attacked the crankshaft oil seal which broke up, letting oil into the clutch.

In fairness to ourselves, I should point out that this unsuccessful outcome was not entirely unexpected, the whole idea having been tried very much as a 'suck it and see' experiment. After a few days, during which we stripped and rebuilt the engine, fitting new seals and a new clutch, the special needles arrived and were quickly fitted.

The engine was warmed up and away we went. One short run was enough to convince us that we had the answer for short sprints. Both torque and bottom-end power were very much increased. We went back to the garage, however, and concentrated now on detail tuning in the quest for even more power. We discovered that, because of the evaporative properties of alcohol, the carburettors and inlet manifold had been icing up. Our answer was to fit a manifold with shorter pipes, bringing the carburettors closer to the warm engine. That prevented further icing, but it necessitated removing the piston dampers to correct the resultant mixture variation.

The mixture was still a little on the rich side, but fortunately throughout the rev range, not just at one end. That showed us that the needle profile was basically correct. We decided next to fit a reverse-cone megaphone exhaust, reasoning that the improved extraction would have the effect of weakening the mixture slightly, as well as providing more power. It worked on both counts and, oh boy, did that vehicle fly! It would pull 8,200rpm easily in all the gears, including top, still using the original final-drive ratio. Top speed was not greatly increased but the acceleration was improved almost beyond belief, 125mph coming up in what seemed no time at all.

Fuel consumption? Well, very high, to put it mildly – we were managing something like two-thirds of a mile per gallon! One further problem arose: the fumes were intolerable, making your eyes and nose stream, giving the driver a sore throat and making everyone cough. All we could do was to keep them out of the car, using adhesive linen tape as a sealer.

How did we shape up at the Brighton Speed trials? Firstly, we were put in the sports and GT class with the Lotuses, Porsches and so on, because the organizers said (rightly) that the car was highly modified and hence outside the saloon category. When it came to the competition, unfortunately, we could have done better. The driver thought the first timed run was another practice and switched the engine off, coasting the last 30 yards over the finish line. Then it rained for the second run!

Nevertheless, the results were still impressive. We were second fastest in class, only three-tenths of a second slower than the winning Lotus, and the second fastest saloon present, Doc Merfield's Cobra-engined Cortina (4.7 litres against our 1.3) being just two-hundredths of a second faster. Our best time for the standing kilometre was 26.48 seconds and our terminal speed was almost 115mph. This was well inside the existing class record and seventh fastest time of the day.

15

Camshafts

The design of the camshaft is one of the most crucial factors determining how an engine performs. Whether it has a fairly even spread of torque or nothing to speak of below 3,500rpm, whether it is a high-revving screamer developing a lot of bhp at the top of the rev range or more of a slogger which will pull from lower revs, these basic characteristics, as well as the bald statistics like the maximum power output available, are controlled to a considerable degree by the camshaft. So there comes a point in tuning a production engine, particularly with competition in mind, when a change of camshaft becomes essential and without it no more performance can be liberated from the unit however much time and money is spent on manifolds, carburettors or head modifications.

But choosing the right camshaft to use can be a daunting prospect for the average enthusiast. There is, it seems, a large and apparently very varied selection on offer, many of which are claimed by their vendors to provide new and previously untapped sources of power. Unfortunately, as with all sales talk, all too often only the virtues are extolled, while the snags remain unmentioned. Many prospective purchasers are incapable of recognizing that snags do even exist, let alone knowing what they are. This is no fault of the enthusiast, for the subject of camshaft design and application is an extremely complex one, all the more so, because, like most aspects of tuning, it is interrelated with many other factors such as cylinder head design and compression ratio,

induction tract shape and fuel system specification, not to mention the possible use of special techniques like supercharging.

With a certain amount of basic knowledge and a little guidance, though, the enthusiast should be better able to make an informed choice, bearing in mind that the advice given earlier about sticking to reputable suppliers applies here with a vengeance.

Let's begin with the basics. As most of you no doubt know already, the function of the camshaft in a four-stroke internal-combustion engine is primarily to provide a mechanical means of opening the inlet and exhaust valves and subsequently allowing them to shut under the influence of the valve springs. For each valve, a cam follower or tappet, either in direct contact with the valve or linked to it by a pushrod and/or rocker, rests against the camshaft, or more accurately the oil film surrounding the camshaft. The portion of the camshaft in question, one of the cams from which it takes its name, is not round but has a distinctive profile, like a modified oval or pear shape. As the camshaft rotates, the follower may be closer or further away from the shaft axis, depending on which part of the cam profile it is in contact with, and in this way the camshaft imparts the required movement to the follower and consequently the valve. When the follower touches the lowest and highest points on the cam, X and Y (see diagram), the valve is respectively fully closed and fully open. Between these points the valve is partially open or closed. Usually points X and Y are slightly 'flattened' (actually truly circular) so that the valve stays fully open or, more particularly, shut for several degrees of camshaft rotation.

Assuming, for the moment, that the rockers (if any) are symmetrical and so do not introduce any extra leverage into the system, you can easily see that the amount by which the valve is opened, the lift, L, is the difference in the distances from the camshaft centre of points X and Y. So either reducing the diameter at X or increasing it at Y, or both, will increase the valve lift.

Since increasing the valve lift, other things being equal, allows more gas to flow into or out of the cylinder, it is basically good news for performance tuning. It does not necessarily decrease engine flexibility (the ability of the engine to perform usefully throughout the rev range and not just flat-out). But the extent to which the lift can be increased is subject to a number of limits. There is the obvious physical dimensional restriction set by the amount of space in the combustion chamber (and increasing that space is counter-productive because it results in a lower compression ratio).

More complex are the limits set by inertia loads. The greater the lift the longer the distance the valve has to move in a given time. If the camshaft (running at half the crankshaft speed, remember) rotates through 360 degrees 4,000 times a minute, the valve travels a distance equivalent to twice the lift (up and down) 4,000 times a minute. Increase the lift by just 0.010in and the valve travels an extra 0.020in every camshaft revolution and an extra 80in per minute.

The trouble is that this imposes much greater stresses on all the components in the valve gear. On top of that, the situation is often aggravated by the fact that tuned engines are usually made to run at higher revs than usual: increasing our camshaft speed from 4,000 to 5,000rpm results in a further 25% increase in the total distance travelled by the valve. You will probably realize that it is not the distance in itself that is the trouble, other than perhaps in terms of its effect on valve guide wear, but the extra acceleration and speed of the valve in travelling these greater distances in a given time.

If 'inertia loads' sounds rather academic, you must try to picture all the reciprocating components of the valve-operating gear being put in motion, made to travel very rapidly in one direction, then stopped, reversed and sent equally rapidly in the other direction – several thousand times a minute. The inertia forces involved when

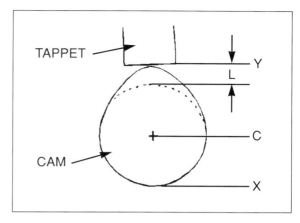

Basic geometry of valve actuation by camshaft. C: camshaft axis. X: lowest part of cam ('base circle'). Y: highest point of cam. Lift imparted to valve, L, equals CY minus CX.

any object is moving do not simply increase in proportion to the speed: they are proportional to the square of the speed, so that doubling the speed increases the force four-fold, trebling the speed increases the force nine-fold, and so on.

Camshaft designers therefore endeavour to compromise by giving the valve as much lift as possible while also giving it as much time as possible, expressed in degrees of camshaft rotation, to travel this distance. One limiting factor there is that, as already mentioned, points X and Y are 'flattened' so that the valve remains fully open and shut for part of its cycle. This double 'dwell' period accounts for a few degrees of camshaft rotation and still further shortens the time and increases the speed of the valve for any given lift.

It is vital, too, to make the cam profile as smooth and progressive as possible within all the other limitations. Abrupt changes in valve direction, from rest to opening or closing, will increase the rate of acceleration of the valve, add to those dreaded inertia loads and encourage the onset of valve bounce. The necessary static clearance in the valve train which we provide by setting the tappet gaps needs to be taken up gently so that the components are not continually hammering against each other. Early camshafts had cams with relatively simple shapes combining just three or four constant-radius curves but the result was a great deal of harshness and noise, and frequent valve-gear breakages when any attempt to use high revs was made. Since those days, a great deal of mathematics has been expended in designing much subtler cam profiles which impart carefully calculated rates of acceleration to the valve gear – it really is a science in its own right, and too complex for these pages.

Those are some of the major mechanical factors affecting camshaft design for the high-performance engine. The other principal aspect of the subject is its effect on the engine's gas-flow characteristics. Cam profiles are not necessarily regular or symmetrical and you will find that the rate of lift imparted to a valve may vary throughout the total opening period: this profiling is related to the position of the piston and to the pressure on the top of the piston at any given position, and often varies from designer to designer. In this area considerations of valve lift, acceleration and overlap come together.

You have all heard about camshafts with large overlap. Briefly, overlap is again measured in degrees of camshaft rotation and indicates the length of time that the inlet and exhaust valves in the same cylinder are open together. While the concept of having both valves open at once may not at first seem to fit very well into the somewhat over-simplified picture most of us have in our head of the operation of the four-stroke cycle, it is in fact necessary for any engine which is required to generate even a relatively modest power output for its capacity. Remember that the process of filling and emptying the cylinders takes place very rapidly – thousands of times per minute at even moderate revs – and that the 'slugs' of gas travelling through the inlet and exhaust tracts are compressible and elastic. The effect of overlap is to allow both the sucking effect of the exhaust leaving the cylinder to help to draw the fresh charge in and the incoming flow to help push the burned residue out. The longer the time that both valves are open the greater will be this effect.

Unfortunately there is once again a limiting snag. The exhaust and inlet gases need to be travelling very quickly for large overlap to have any useful effect. The condition does apply on all engines even at low speeds but only for a very short time each cycle. If we were to use a camshaft with a lot of overlap on a normal road engine driven at 2,000rpm, we would find inlet gases escaping through the exhaust valve and exhaust gases flowing back through the inlet valve. This is why a full-race engine has no power low down in the rev range and often refuses altogether to idle slowly.

As engine speed rises, the gas speed rises too, and the intermittent and sometimes reversible flow gradually smooths out until the engine comes 'on the cam'. At this point there is no reversal of flow and both inlet and exhaust gases pass quickly and efficiently in the correct direction. Camshafts for racing engines, where neither low-speed running nor economy are of any import, are usually designed to allow the exhaust gases to be completely pushed out by the incoming charge, even to the point where some of the fresh mixture escapes down the exhaust just before the valve closes. Overlap and combustion chamber design need to be related, since the shape of the chamber has a bearing on how quickly and thoroughly it can be filled or emptied. A chamber with lots of nooks and crannies tends to retain pockets of gas which cannot easily be exhausted or even ignited.

Overlap is also related to exhaust manifold design and a poorly designed exhaust manifold can prevent the use of a high-overlap camshaft. Although overlap refers to the amount of time both inlet and exhaust valves in the same cylinder are open, a long overlap also means that exhaust valves on different cylinders may be open together. With a short-branch manifold, it is possible for exhaust gasses to shoot back up an adjacent branch and into a different cylinder – most upsetting!

In summary, high lift and long overlap are both desirable features of a camshaft for a high-performance engine, but both are limited by other factors, principal among which are firstly the mechanical strength of the valve gear and related components and secondly the need to make the engine function satisfactorily at speeds other than flat-out. And there are a lot of other interrelated considerations as well. It quickly becomes very clear that camshaft design is an extremely complex and specialized subject. We have only looked at the most basic principles, and to go further would need several large and complicated volumes full of advanced mathematics which are beyond me anyway.

But what does all this mean to you and me if we are trying to decide which camshaft to buy for our lovingly tuned engine? Firstly, as with a lot of decisions about tuning, we need to consider what the car is going to be used for. If granny wants to use it for shopping or you are regularly using it to teach someone to drive, then you must use a standard camshaft. Other tuning procedures can still be applied, in moderation, to result in a faster car which is pleasanter to drive, but the flexibility, freedom from temperament, and good manners around town will be maintained. Fast road use and the milder forms of rallying do not demand such flexible or durable engines so that camshafts with a moderate increase in lift and overlap can be used. Normally these will not pose the kind of mechanical problems which can arise with a really diabolical, out-and-out full-race camshaft, and it is with those problems that I am mostly concerned. The following points apply to all replacement camshafts to some extent, but most particularly to the full-race type.

Some tuning specialists offer reground camshafts, which are in fact often standard camshafts with the cams modified in shape. To regrind a camshaft of course means removing metal, and unfortunately all too often this results in a most unsubtle profile with violent transitions causing tremendous valve acceleration, and necessitating very, very strong valve springs. Personally, I do not like most of the regrinds that I have seen and, at risk of raising a storm (because of course there are notable exceptions), my advice is avoid regrinds of standard camshafts and stick to purpose-made performance components like the BMC 731 cam.

Many standard camshafts do not have enough metal in them to allow them to be changed from mild to wild specification and retain reliability: the finished shape is not the only important factor. So camshafts which are based on specially made blanks are a much better buy. For example, even the old BMC 544, when manufactured as such, was a really good cam, but regrinds from more standard cams to the 544 specification were the cause of many broken valves and suffered from pitting of the cam faces and various other troubles. The same can be said of the later 649 cam.

Related to the choice of camshaft is the question of changing the valve springs. With increased valve lift and higher revs, both basic ploys of the tuner looking for an increase in power output, the danger of valve bounce is increased. It's those inertia loads again. To take the extreme case, if the highest point on the cam profile were literally a point, even a non-engineer can understand intuitively that it would be completely impossible to keep the cam follower in continuous contact with the cam: the follower, pushrod, rocker, valve and spring would all tend to go on travelling in the 'valve opening' direction as the point passed. Eventually, of course, the spring would bring them to a halt and catapult them back in the opposite direction to send the cam follower

crashing into contact with the cam again.

Even well short of that extreme, of course, an increase in maximum engine revs and/or the use of a camshaft with a more vigorous profile can produce valve bounce. The instantaneous loads on the valve gear can be enormous, and the impact of the follower on the cam may well damage the highly finished surfaces of both components and precipitate rapid wear. The valves may be bouncing off their seats at the wrong point in the combustion cycle, leading to burnt valves and damaged seats. Contact between a valve and the rising piston is possible in bad cases, and there are few quicker ways of wrecking the engine.

So valve bounce is potentially very dangerous: to prevent its onset, it becomes necessary to use stronger valve springs. But if the process is carried too far, reliability problems set in. As you will realize, the action of a valve spring is to exert a pull along the length of a valve stem: so theoretically a strong enough spring could stretch the valve stem like elastic or pull it apart like putty. Since valve movement is limited by the valve seat in the cylinder head, the valve head could be pulled right through the seat or break up by turning inside out like an umbrella.

Of course those are extremes which do not normally happen, and never when the engine is stationary. But with the engine running at, say, 8,000rpm the forces involved are greatly increased, and the valve is subjected to great stress from rapidly changing high temperatures too. So failure, most commonly in the region of the valve spring locating collar, can occur. Also, even if the valve is strong enough to withstand these forces, it remains true that to open the valve the camshaft must push against the spring, and the greater the pressure required the greater the stress in the whole valve-operating train. Rapid wear, even pitting and surface deterioration of the cam faces and breakage of the cam followers can result. Aside from damage, the stronger the springs the greater the power consumed in opening them and consequently subtracted from the power available to propel the car. Springs, then, should be chosen to be as weak as is adequate, and certainly not on the basis of as strong as possible.

So it makes sense to reduce as far as possible the need for an increase in valve spring strength. Besides choosing a camshaft of good design, how is this best to be done? Lightening the reciprocating parts of the valve gear is the main method open to us, and there are more details in the next chapter.

Camshafts for the A-series engine

Returning now to our specific subject, the A-series engine, there have been over the years quite a number of different camshafts produced by the manufacturer for this power unit, either as standard equipment or as part of the factory tuning programme. There is a good deal of interchangeability between them and some of the possible swaps have been mentioned earlier in the book. The question of the different types of oil-pump drive is covered in a later chapter. Here, we will look first at the various camshafts likely to be chosen for tuning purposes and then at what can and cannot be used in the case of each specific engine variant. As a general principle, remember that the smaller the engine capacity the more it will tend to lose usable bottom-end power with a wild camshaft.

First, a brief word on regrinds. It is only when chasing the last half a brake horsepower with a racing engine that one need even contemplate modifying a camshaft supplied by the manufacturer's tuning department, and most people still use an ordinary 648/649 cam for racing. Avoid any supposed race-specification regrind which is not based on the 648/649 camshaft (part number C-AEA 648). This, providing it is done properly, can be slightly modified: normally, little metal need be removed as it already has a fair amount of lift and overlap, neither of which can be radically increased. Further, any reground camshaft should have been treated to harden it, by a process such as nitriding or Tuftriding – it will be effectively useless without. But even this has its problems in that it can cause distortion, and any treated regrind must be carefully checked for this.

AEA 630 Really only worth fitting on the 850 Mini as a fairly mild road camshaft. Gives excellent bottom-end power even with an 848cc engine, but must not be taken over 6,000 to 6,200rpm as it imparts dangerously high acceleration to the inlet valve gear. Little top-end power.

AEG 148 Similar to AEA 630 in most respects.

88G229 Formerly known as 2A948. A mild rally camshaft which works works quite well on all engines but does destroy bottom-end power on 848cc Minis. Runs out of power at about 6,500rpm. It has the advantage of being cheap and easy to obtain, and it is not too harsh on valve gear.

AEG 510 I have little experience of this cam but I would say that one can expect results very similar to those obtained with the 88G229 camshaft.

The effects of the camshafts listed so far are pretty slight and many people don't even bother to change the standard article for one of these. Could be useful if you are rebuilding an engine anyway, though. The 88G229 is probably the most widely used and often regarded as the old faithful. Next, we come to the 'diabolical' camshafts, and the competition-orientated enthusiast begins to take notice.

C-AEA 731 This really is a fabulous 'Jack of all trades'. It can be regarded as a vigorous rally or semi-race camshaft. It is also good for the really keen road man who is prepared to put up with little tick-over and little power low down. But in a properly tuned engine it gives excellent power from around 3,500rpm and goes on giving power to 7,000-plus. It is not too hard on the valve gear.

C-AEA 648 Often referred to as the 649. An out-and-out full-race camshaft. No power below 5,000rpm (perhaps 4,000 to 4,500 in some cases) and power in plenty up to 8,500-plus. Lift too great for ordinary unmodified valve-head assembly and will cause spring crush. Needs Cooper S-length valves, or spring locating grooves machined away to expose more valve stem: the easiest way is to use Cooper S valves with the heads turned down to size if necessary. This camshaft is very hard on valve gear, especially cam followers. It replaces the old 544 camshaft which was discontinued. If using any of the cams not originally designed for the Cooper S in an S engine, one must modify the projecting slotted shaft of the oil pump.

C-AEG 529 Identical to the 648/649 but has a different oil-pump drive to suit the spline-driven pump on the non-S 1,275cc Sprite/Midget/1300 engine.

C-AEG 595, C-AEG 597 Two later camshafts originally designed for the fuel-injection version of the racing 1275 Cooper S engine. Both have the spline-type oil-pump drive. Both are reputed to have the same amount of lift as the 648/649 and 529, but differ in having different periods of valve opening and overlaps. The milder of the two, C-AEG 597, has an inlet period of 320 degrees and an exhaust period of 300 degrees. The hotter, C-AEG 595, has periods of 320 degrees for both inlet and exhaust. Thus both are more extreme than the 648/649/529 cams which have periods of 300 degrees for both inlet and exhaust. Both these later camshafts have less bottom-end power but it is to be hoped that they will increase an engine's top-end output.

I must stress that all the racing camshafts mentioned make very heavy demands on valve

En route to a famous victory: Rauno Aaltonen and Henry Liddon on their way to winning the 1967 Monte Carlo Rally, one of the pinnacles of the Mini's sporting career.

Equally at home on the race track: this is Alec Poole's very successful Equipe Arden Cooper S.

A-series camshaft details

	C1	C2	C3	C4	C5	C6	C7	C8	C9	C10
Part number/s *(pin-drive oil pump)*	8G 712 / 2A 297 / 2A 571	12G 165 / AEA 630	AEG 148	88G 229 / 2A 948	AEG 510	C-AEA 731	C-AEA 544	C-AEA 648	—	—
Marking	—	2 rings	—	1 ring	1 ring	3 rings	AEA 544	AEA 649	—	—
Standard use*	A	B	C	D	E	L	M	L	—	—
Part number/s *(spline-drive oil pump)*	12A 1065	12G 726	AEG 522 / AEG 537	C-AEG 567	C-AEG 542	—	—	C-AEG 529	C-AEG 597	C-AEG 595
Marking	—	2 rings	—	AEG 567	AEG 543	—	—	AEG 530	AEG 598	AEG 596
Standard use*	F	G	H	J	K	L	—	L	L	L
Cam lobe width (in)	3/8	3/8	1/2	3/8	1/2	3/8	1/2	1/2	1/2	1/2
Inlet opens BTDC (deg)	5	5	5	16	10	24	34	50	60	60
Inlet closes ABDC (deg)	45	45	45	56	50	64	74	70	80	80
Exhaust opens BBDC (deg)	40	51	51	51	51	59	69	75	75	85
Exhaust closes ATDC (deg)	10	21	21	21	21	29	39	45	45	55
Inlet period (deg)	230	230	230	252	240	268	288	300	320	320
Exhaust period (deg)	230	252	252	252	252	268	288	300	300	320
Cam lift (in)	0.221	0.250	0.250	0.250	0.250	0.252	0.306	0.315	0.315	0.315
Valve lift (in)	0.285	0.318	0.318	0.318	0.318	0.320	0.388	0.394	0.394	0.394
Running clearance (in)	0.012	0.012	0.012	0.015	0.015	0.015	0.015	0.015	0.015	0.015
Timing clearance (in)	0.019	0.019	0.021	0.019	0.021	0.021	0.021	0.021	0.021	0.021

*Standard applications

A: Mini 850 and 998, Sprite Mk1.

B: 1100 range, Cooper 998, Sprite Mk2 and Midget Mk1 (948cc).

C: Early Cooper S, Sprite Mk3 and Midget Mk2 (1,098cc with 2in main bearings).

D: Cooper 997.

E: Cooper S from 9FSAY-4006.

F: Automatic Mini 850 and 998.

G: Automatic 1100.

H: Sprite Mk4 and Midget Mk3 (1,275cc)

J: Mild competition.

K: Rally road.

L: Racing.

M: Early full race.

Light weight and 'chuckable' handling made the Mini a good rallycross car. More solutions to the twin problems of seeing through the screen and keeping the bonnet shut!

gear reliability. It is essential to check dimensions to ensure that spring crush will not occur. High-quality springs are a must, and if the valves themselves are not made of best quality racing Nimonic materials they will almost certainly break after a short period of use. I would therefore use nothing other than Nimonic valves from the Special Tuning department or other reputable supplier. It may be necessary to use longer tappet adjusting screws, or to machine 0.050in from the bases of the rocker shaft pedestals, to obtain the correct angularity between rockers and valve stem tips. With extra strong Cooper S valve springs, the special bottom locating cups as supplied by the Special Tuning department are required.

Let us now look at camshaft choice in relation to each of the various A-series engines. Inevitably, there are a number of interdependent factors to consider in each case, principal among which is the safe rev limit imposed on the engine by components such as the crankshaft and connecting rods. Most of the hotter camshafts are of real benefit only towards the top end of the rev range.

848cc engine. The maximum safe revs on this engine are 6,000 to 6,500rpm providing one ignores the timing chain life – the standard chain tensioner disintegrates at about 5,500rpm. Some people wisely advocate less than this and set 6,000rpm as a regular limit, and I am one of them. Personally, I reckon a standard cam is all right for road use or an AEA 630 for rallying. On the other hand, if one carefully builds up an 850 engine to racing standards then one can use 7,500 and very occasionally 8,000rpm with reasonable if not complete safety, which enables one to use the C-AEA 648 camshaft with suitable valves and springs. Such an engine would be totally useless on the road, and if road use is envisaged you must not go beyond the 731 camshaft. By racing standards I mean using the latest crankshaft, fitted with a vibration damper, and fully balancing the engine. Remember that any camshaft change on this engine, as well as using stronger valve springs allowing 6,500rpm or more, must be accompanied by line-boring the camshaft housing and fitting bearing liners, and that means a complete engine strip-down. Camshaft seizure and a wrecked engine is the penalty for omitting this vital step.

948cc engine. I would consider this engine in exactly the same light as the 850 except that I would use the 88G229 camshaft as my mildest improvement rather than the AEA 630. This engine also needs to have the camshaft housing line-bored and fitted with bearing liners.

Paddy Hopkirk and Henry Liddon on the ascent of Mont Ventoux during the 1963 Tour de France in which they scored a first in class and third place overall.

997cc engine. Used only in the early Coopers. Fully prepared, capable of 7,200 to 7,500rpm. This was the first engine fitted with camshaft bearing liners as standard. The 2A948 camshaft was standard equipment. I would not use the C-AEA 648 cam in this case, limiting myself to the 731 (or, if available, the older 544 camshaft). This is not because in standard form this engine is any less reliable than the 848cc or 948cc engines, in fact the reverse is true, but this is now an obsolete engine which means that it can no longer be developed to the same extent as versions which continued for much longer.

998cc engine. Somewhat better than the 997cc engine, having a better bore to stroke ratio (shorter stroke) and rather better reliability. The 998 Cooper used the AEA 630 camshaft as standard. The 88G229 is an excellent road-cum-rally improvement, bearing in mind my earlier comment. Some people still race this engine or derivatives from it. With a safe limit of 7,500rpm and occasional use of 8,000, the C-AEA 648 camshaft is an excellent fitting for that purpose, with, of course, suitable valves, springs and other appropriate modifications.

1,098cc engine. This engine comes in two forms, the later version (Mk3 Sprite and Mk2 Midget) having a more rigid block and 2in diameter main-bearing journals to distinguish it from the earlier Spridget and transverse 1100 version. Maximum revs on the weaker version should be kept below 6,500rpm. I would never suggest anything more vigorous than an 88G229 camshaft: if you use, say, a 731 or 649 and take advantage of the extra power then, as sure as eggs is eggs, there will be an almighty bang! The 1,098cc engine with the strengthening modifications is a rather different proposition, however, and, providing you fit the special BLMC competition crankshaft, it becomes very reliable. Any camshaft is usable then, though I would limit my choice to the 731 or the 649.

970, 1,071 and 1,275cc S engines. I have lumped these three together because basically they can be considered as identical for purposes of camshaft selection. The standard camshafts are, of course, hotter than those of more mundane Minis, though still not exactly wild. The 731 makes an excellent general-purpose camshaft, and the 649 is ideal for competition, having been designed for the Cooper S in the first place.

1,275cc non-S engine. As fitted to late Spridgets, 1300s and 1275 GT Minis. This engine is limited to camshafts equipped to take the splined oil-pump drive (more details in Chapter 17) such as the C-AEG 529 (similar to 649), C-AEG 542 (similar to 731), C-AEG 595 and C-AEG 597.

16

Lightening valve gear

By reducing the weight of components in the valve gear, as we have already seen, the inertia loads are reduced, which is in itself beneficial in terms of reducing wear and tear, and either the onset of valve bounce is postponed to higher engine speeds (and hopefully beyond the useful rev range) or alternatively the strength of valve spring needed to prevent bounce is reduced. Though aimed at the A-series unit, the following notes on lightening valve gear apply in general terms to almost any engine with pushrod-operated overhead valves.

Starting at the camshaft end of the valve operating train, we find the cylindrical or bucket-shaped cam followers or tappets. These are specially case hardened at manufacture and this makes their modification by ordinary hand tools almost impossible. I always take mine to a good machinist who modifies them to my specification on a lathe at no great expense. I have the overall length reduced by ⅛in. The inside is then machined out to reduce the wall thickness, tapering to almost eggshell dimensions at the open top end, at the same time ensuring that the bottom has a nicely blended internal radius into the base to minimize the possibility of the base breaking away from the side walls.

These machining operations have a useful secondary function. Something like 20% of all A-series cam followers turn out to be unsuitable for use in a racing engine because they are over-hardened and too brittle, but this is almost impossible to discern until you try to machine them. Those that are too hard cannot be machined, they just crack or break the cutting tool, and they must be thrown away. So to make up a full set of nine followers, one being a spare, you will probably need to start with a dozen. Don't send the over-hardened ones back to the makers under warranty: they are perfectly all right for road use, and you will just get laughed at. They are not designed for racing use, or at least their final inspection process isn't.

In an earlier edition of *Tuning the Mini*, I suggested that one could machine a flat on the outside of each tappet to increase oil splash and lubrication of the valve gear. That was based on the tappets found in a 'works' engine purchased by myself in the early days of Mini tuning. This must *not* be done. The size and shape of the base of the tappet is part of the geometry of the whole valve train and in part determines the opening period of the valve: since tappets rotate in their bores when the engine is running, an irregularly-shaped base will cause irregular valve opening. Looking back, I am amazed that such experienced tuners as those who produced that engine had apparently failed to realize this.

Next in the valve operating train come the pushrods. It used to be fashionable for suppliers to advertise outstanding properties of lightness and strength for light alloy pushrods. In fact, not only do they lack the strength and rigidity of their steel counterparts, size for size, but the extent to which they expand and contract with changes in temperature makes them worse than useless.

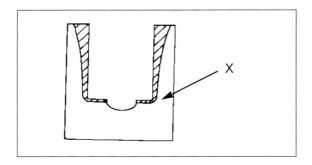

The cam followers or tappets can be lightened by removing metal from the internal areas shown shaded. Ensure that there is a smooth radius between internal wall and base at X.

Tappet settings become meaningless. There is no substitute for steel, except perhaps titanium which is very, very expensive.

Some people have successfully used tubular steel pushrods (in fact some other engine designs have them as standard) but although I was once a great believer in them, I am not so sure these days: I feel that they lack rigidity and increase valve-gear flexing which is very detrimental. It's yet another problem, of course, which is made worse by more vigorous cam profiles. So I think it best to stick to the standard article, lightened.

The only places where metal can be removed are at the ends, from around the foot and the top cup. The latter can be machined on the outside to reduce the overall size and thickness. On no account must you remove metal from the inside of the cup. The foot can be reduced by removing metal from the uppermost portion. Metal must not be removed from the contact area under the foot. This work can all be done freehand using a bench-mounted grinder or a large abrasive disc, but it is rather tedious and considerable care is needed to avoid 'necking' the rod at the points where the cup and foot join the shank. That greatly weakens the rod and necessitates its replacement. I have done it freehand but ended up needing several spare rods to replace the 'necked' ones. Better, then, that this operation should be performed on a lathe as it is then very simple and hence cheap.

Most people associate valve-gear lightening with the removal of metal from the rockers alone, often ignoring all the other parts. Although it is advantageous to reduce weight in all the reciprocating components of the valve train, it is true that the greatest reductions are often made in the rockers, providing they have sufficient reserves of strength and are made of cast, not

pressed, steel. The pressed steel type must be replaced if at all possible. Often one can find that different models using basically similar engines have different rockers and a better pattern can be found. For the Mini, the later Cooper S rockers, part number AEG 425, are the perfect example of this. To be interchangeable, of course, they must have the same principal dimensions, including the ratio of leverage (the effective lengths of the two halves of the rocker, which are not always equal).

The most effective savings in rocker weight are in those areas which travel the greatest distance, consequently reach the highest speeds and are subject to the greatest acceleration, the extreme ends. Fortunately these are also the areas which are least subject to breakage. Taking the valve stem end of the rocker first, this is usually a solid rectangular lump of metal, obviously far heavier than it need be, with the excess material in the width of the pad, not the depth. One reason for this excess width is that it compensates for any inaccuracies in the alignment of the rocker over the valve stem – the rocker can wander about on its shaft and still make contact with the valve. If one knows that the rockers align accurately, because the springs on the shaft have been replaced by spacers as suggested in Chapter 2, then the pad can be reduced in width almost to the diameter of the valve stem. If, on the other hand, alignment is uncertain or inaccurate, then the bottom of the pad which contacts the valve must not be narrowed, but the pad can still be lightened by tapering its width higher up.

On no account must metal be removed from the sole of the pad: this is machined to a radius so that although the rocker moves in an arc the pressure on the valve remains vertical, in line with the length of the valve stem, throughout the movement. Any inaccuracy in that radius will put side thrust forces on the valve stem, tending to bend it and to wear the guide out rapidly. Apart from anything else, this also means that worn rockers should not be 'reclaimed' by grinding the contact surface of the pad: they must be replaced.

At the adjuster end of the rocker, there is often a large lump of weld and/or ridges left in the casting. Obviously these should both be removed. Sometimes removal of the weld uncovers an oilway drilling which it was intended to blank off: in my opinion it is relatively unimportant whether this hole be closed with a little solder or plastic metal, or simply left open.

The rounded, internally threaded section of the rocker which houses the adjuster can have its

Rockers of the pressed steel type, left, are not suitable for lightening and should be replaced by the cast pattern, right.

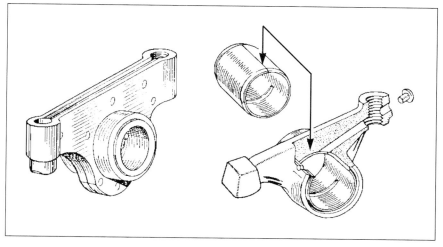

Rockers are lightened by removing metal from the unstressed areas at the ends. The depth of the central part of the rocker gives it the necessary beam strength and must not be reduced.

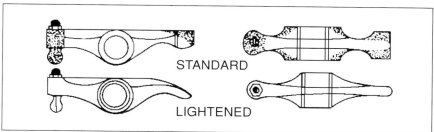

STANDARD

LIGHTENED

outside diameter reduced by an amount which will depend on the original thickness, using common sense as a guide to leaving sufficient strength. I usually make this outside diameter approximately the same as that of the locking nut used on the adjuster screw. The bottom edge of the rounded section can be bevelled off, but the top must continue to provide a flat surface for the nut to lock against otherwise the adjuster will work loose.

You will often find that the adjuster screw has a very deep screwdriver slot in it, the depth of which can be reduced by removing metal from the top of the screw. The locking nuts often have part numbers or trade marks embossed on them which can be removed for very small savings – every little helps! It is possible to reduce the ball of the adjuster screw to a pear shape, but since it is a very hard material a precision grinder is needed for good results and I don't usually bother with this. All the other work can be carried out with simple hand tools, perhaps augmented by a bench grinder or abrasive discs.

You can polish and smooth the whole surface of the rocker but the weight reduction to be achieved is very small and it is doubtful whether

the effect would be discernibly better than a rocker which has simply been properly lightened at the ends. Such intricate finishing and polishing is very time consuming.

You must remember that rockers are subject to very high stresses and no attempt should be made to reduce the depth of a rocker at any point other than the very ends which can be bevelled off. A rocker relies on its depth for its beam strength in the vertical plane in which it is loaded, and strength should never be sacrificed for lightness – unless you are a stress calculations genius! Trial and error could be very expensive.

It is not really possible to lighten the valve spring retaining collars and collets of the A-series engine and retain adequate strength. Dural collars are often used on motorcycles and I imagine they would provide very worthwhile weight savings if you could get them made up. I wish I had the guts to try them but, oh boy, what a disaster if they broke at 8,500rpm!

The camshaft-mounted timing chain sprocket can be lightened by machining and drilling, providing it is of the Cooper S steel type. But this merely reduces the load on the timing chain and camshaft: it's not part of the reciprocating gear

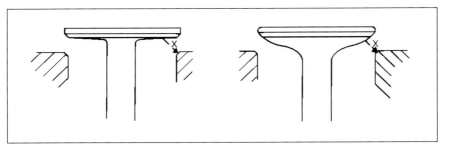

The 'penny-on-a-stick' valve shape, left, allows a wider gap, X, between valve and seat when open than the tulip shape does, right, and has the additional advantage of lighter weight.

and so has no influence on valve bounce or spring strength.

The only parts of the valve train we have not so far talked about are the valves themselves. The inlet valves can be significantly lightened as a by-product of reshaping them to improve gas flow. The 'penny-on-a-stick' shape, as explained earlier in the book, is chosen as best suiting the gas-flow characteristics of the A-series engine, but it has the secondary advantage of reducing the mass of metal in the valve. For that reason also, it should not be applied to the exhaust valve where the greater mass of metal is necessary to withstand the high temperatures to which it is subjected.

I have often been asked why the apparently more 'streamlined' tulip shape is not better for gas flow. Basically, the reason is this. Tulip valves work very well on cylinder heads which have a straight port into the combustion chamber, for example the downdraught type, especially if the combustion chamber is hemispherical and the edge of the valve is not immediately adjacent to the chamber wall. On the A-series engine, however, we find a sidedraught port with a sharp bend in it, followed by a short run into the combustion chamber through the valve throat. The edge of the valve comes very close to the chamber wall. Together,

these features mean that the gas-flow pattern is at best still some way from ideal.

Where the incoming gases can shoot straight into the cylinder, a streamlined valve shape which offers the least resistance is preferable. But with our already impeded gas flow, the charge tends to spread into the cylinder under and around the valve, and the size of the ring-shaped opening between the valve seat and the open valve becomes a more important factor. As can be seen from the diagram, the clear area at full lift is greater with the 'penny-on-a-stick' shape, and the difference is even more marked at, say, half lift. The tulip shape in fact reduces the gap between the valve and seat and so reduces the total amount of fuel mixture which it is possible to get into the cylinder – exactly the reverse of what we are aiming at when tuning an engine.

That the 'penny-on-a-stick' valve is also a lot lighter is an added bonus. Tulip valves are sometimes lightened by hollowing the heads, but this not only increases the combustion chamber volume, which is unacceptable on something like an 850 Mini where it is already difficult enough to get the volume down to create a high enough compression ratio, but also makes nasty little pockets in which unburnt gases can collect.

17

Changing oil pumps

The A-series engine has the oil pump driven directly from the end of the camshaft. In most versions, the coupling takes the form of a pin through the hollow end of the camshaft which engages in a slot in the pump shaft. With the introduction of the 1,275cc Sprite/Midget engine and then the non-S 1300 transverse unit, a new drive arrangement appeared: the pump shaft is splined and meshes with a splined drive washer which in turn has three lugs on its outer edge to engage in three slots machined in the hollow end of the camshaft. This later set-up is generally reckoned to be stronger and more reliable. With the earlier pin drive, it is not unknown for the pump shaft to shear when starting the engine from cold, a problem particularly prevalent with engines developing 100psi oil pressure and using thick, castor-based oil. To swap from one design to the other, however, is not entirely straightforward.

The change in design means that there are two basic pump types which are of interest to the enthusiast. For brevity, these can be called splined pumps and pin pumps. Pin pumps are themselves divided into two types, one being used on the Cooper S, the other on all other non-1300 A-series units. The S pump has a longer rotor shaft because of the extra length of the S block. The same extra length is a feature of the non-S 1300 block. (There is another type of pump fitted to the automatic Mini which need not concern us here.)

So much for the background, what about the practicalities of fitting the splined pump to a non-1300 engine? Two snags are evident. Firstly, the camshafts are not interchangeable, as the tail end is differently machined for the spline drive. Secondly, the pin pump is retained by three bolts whereas the splined pump is fixed by four similar but shorter bolts.

In the case of the Cooper S, all that is necessary to fit the later pump is to drill and tap two extra holes into the block to accept the extra bolts, and choose the appropriate camshaft. With these conditions met, it merely becomes a matter of bolting the whole lot together. With the introduction of the C-AEG 595 and 597 camshafts, both with increased valve opening periods compared with the 649 cam and both designed for spider pump drive, fitting the later pump has become quite common.

It is when you come to apply the spline-drive set-up to other A-series engines that the real problems arise, as I found out when I came to do it on my 850 racer. As with the Cooper S, two extra tapped holes were needed in the block. When I came to fit the whole lot together, I found that the camshaft, fully located, protruded from the front of the block by about 0.275in, or 0.225in more than it should. I had in fact expected this, because the pump was designed to suit the extra block length of either type of 1,275cc engine. What was happening was that the splined pump shaft was sliding right through the splined washer so that the boss on the pump body fouled the washer and pushed the camshaft forward in the block.

I certainly couldn't just grind the required amount off the front end of the camshaft, even given the necessary equipment for the job, because the bearing oilways in cam and block would no longer align, a sure recipe for oil starvation and a major blow-up. I decided that the only way out was to remove metal from the drive washer and the pump boss. Accordingly, I ground 0.100in off the washer, making it thinner, and took 0.125in off the pump boss, making it shorter. On reassembly, I found that the camshaft now only stuck out at the front of the block by the required 0.050in.

However, another problem manifested itself. Although the pump boss no longer fouled the drive washer, I found that the splines in the latter no longer mated with those on the pump shaft. The splined part of the shaft had passed almost right through the washer and contact was only being made by the very ends of the splines: in use this would cause the splines to shear and result in drive failure. But what I regard as a design fault in the pump allowed me to overcome this difficulty.

The splined shaft is merely a press fit in the pump rotor and, by setting it up in a vice, I was able to push the shaft back into the rotor a distance of 0.225in, the excess amount by which

the camshaft had originally protruded. Then 0.225in was ground off the tail end of the shaft so that it could seat properly in the pump body. Much to my relief, it all fitted together this time, and the engine ran satisfactorily.

I do not think that these modifications reduce reliability in any way. The area over which the drive washer and shaft make contact is more than adequate and almost certainly still stronger than the earlier pin drive arrangement. The reduction in the shaft bearing area, brought about by shortening the pump boss, is negligible, particularly since it is swamped with oil. The spline drive works as a kind of universal joint too, eliminating, or at least greatly reducing, any side-thrust loadings on the shaft or bearing.

An alternative way to fit a spline-drive pump to a small-capacity block is to use a spacer of the appropriate thickness between pump and block. If you can obtain the spacer ready made, this makes the job simplicity itself. If you contemplate manufacturing the spacer yourself, remember that it must mate accurately with pump and block, and not obstruct the oilways: any deficiency could result in loss of oil pressure.

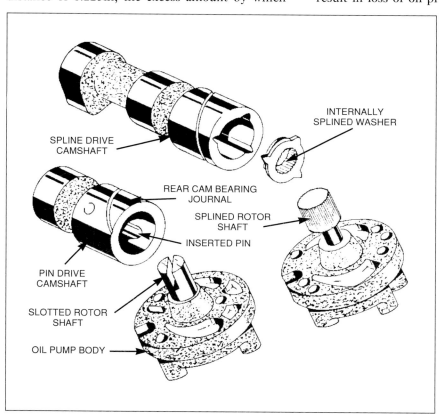

INTERNALLY SPLINED WASHER

SPLINE DRIVE CAMSHAFT

REAR CAM BEARING JOURNAL

SPLINED ROTOR SHAFT

INSERTED PIN

PIN DRIVE CAMSHAFT

SLOTTED ROTOR SHAFT

OIL PUMP BODY

Pin-drive and spline-drive oil pumps and camshafts compared.

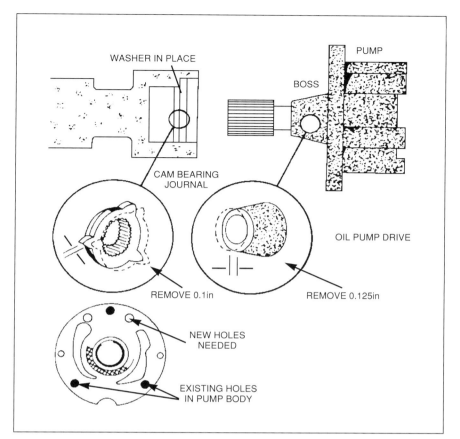

WASHER IN PLACE

PUMP

BOSS

CAM BEARING
JOURNAL

OIL PUMP DRIVE

REMOVE 0.1in

REMOVE 0.125in

NEW HOLES
NEEDED

EXISTING HOLES
IN PUMP BODY

Fitting a spline-drive pump and camshaft to an 850 engine meant thinning the drive washer, shortening the pump boss and drilling two new bolt holes in the block.

Rearward aspect of a Mk2 Mini-Cooper S, showing the revised rear lamp units, and fillers for the twin fuel tanks which were standard equipment after 1966.

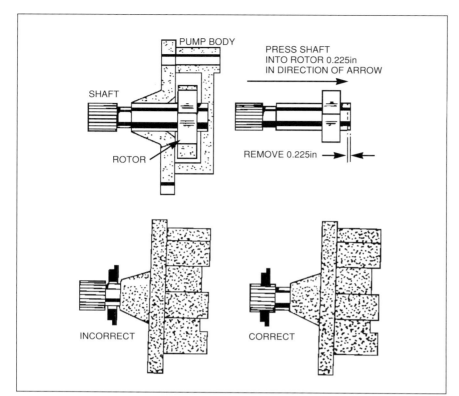

PUMP BODY

PRESS SHAFT
INTO ROTOR 0.225in
IN DIRECTION OF ARROW

SHAFT

ROTOR

REMOVE 0.225in →

INCORRECT

CORRECT

Internal pump modifications involved pressing the shaft through the rotor by 0.225in and removing an equal amount from the end of the shaft. This was necessary to ensure the correct location of the drive washer on the splines.

Two incidental points emerge from the preceding; firstly, that I was using one of the latest camshafts in my 850 racer, and secondly, that I considered the pump to have a design fault. On the first count, I later reverted to a 649 cam, for the later C-AEG 597 gave results no better than with the 649 on this particular engine and, in addition, needed about 14 degrees static advance on a Cooper S distributor. I felt that to run an engine with that much advance spelt trouble – 10 degrees static advance on this distributor is more than enough.

On the second count, I don't think the pump will give trouble either on 850 racers, which only develop 85 or 90psi oil pressure, or on any other engine using thin, mineral oils. But it seems to me that a pump shaft which is only an unkeyed press fit in the pump rotor could easily cause problems on engines using castor-based oil which are very thick when cold. I think that under those circumstances the forces applied to the pump might cause the shaft to rotate in the rotor without turning it. But it would not be too difficult to drill and pin the rotor to the shaft to eliminate this danger.

There was one other minor snag in fitting the splined pump to my particular 850 engine. The pump body is externally slightly larger than the earlier type and I found that it fouled against the bell-housing. A couple of minutes with a file soon put that right, however. Some later bell-housings have small cut-aways to give sufficient clearance, but the difference is not enough to warrant the cost of a new housing.

18

Ignition and generator

An efficient and reliable ignition system is vital to an engine's performance. Probably the commonest causes of poor running and unreliable starting are to be found in the electrics. With a tuned car, therefore, it is imperative that the ignition system is functioning as near perfectly as possible, otherwise a proportion of the effort and expense put into improving the performance is simply wasted. The basics of ignition maintenance and adjustment are too familiar to need repetition here, so I need not remind you (need I?) that plugs and points should be free from excessive deposits and set exactly to the recommended gaps. The points should be ground flat and adjusted to mate squarely with each other over the entire surface: replace them if that cannot be achieved.

The entire electrical system should be clean and free from dirt and grease, though it is advisable to apply a little clean grease or water repellent to joints and connectors to keep water out. But beyond regular maintenance, what changes to standard specification are useful for enhanced performance?

Sparking plugs

Most highly stressed of all the ignition components are the sparking plugs. Enthusiastic drivers rarely use their cars in a manner conducive to long life of the maker's standard plugs. Usually these plugs are very soft (hot running) and are easily burned out. Often it is essential that a grade of plug at least slightly harder (colder running) is fitted, say N3 instead of N5 in the Champion range. Failure to do this can lead to rapid plug burning or even complete breakdown, causing misfiring. The more highly tuned an engine, the higher the revs, the higher the compression ratio, then the harder the plugs need to be.

For more extreme circumstances it may, in addition, prove necessary to fit a different type of plug, changing perhaps from extended nose to standard gap or even, on a racing engine, recessed-nose racing plugs. Generally speaking, recessed-nose plugs are toughest and have most resistance to wear. Standard gap comes second in this respect, while extended-nose plugs have, comparatively, least wear resistance. Combine the varying grades of hardness and the different plug types and you can see that there is plenty of variety and there should be no difficulty in finding a plug exactly suited to your requirements.

Because 'hard plugs' have become synonymous with high performance, some people have been tempted to over-do the business of changing to a harder grade. It is true that if an over-soft plug burns out, say under racing conditions, the consequences can include a dropped electrode and a holed piston. But the ideal is a plug just hard enough, not the hardest possible that will make the engine run. The harder the plugs, the easier it will be to wet them at low speeds and the more difficult the engine will be to start from cold – damage may even result from repeated cold starting. So for general use a compromise becomes necessary. The sparking-plug manufacturers' application lists will often be a useful guide.

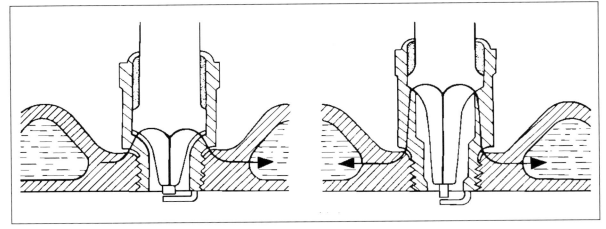

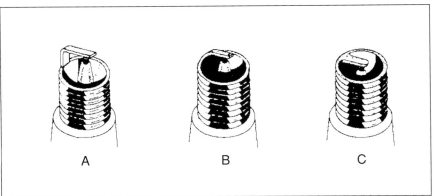

Cross-section of cold (left) and hot (right) plugs. The colder plug has a shorter ceramic insulator nose and provides a shorter path for heat dissipation.

Three types of sparking plug: A extended nose; B standard gap; C recessed nose.

Ignition coil

Tuning the engine does not, as some people seem to think, immediately make it necessary to fit a sports/racing coil. The standard Mini or Cooper coil is entirely adequate for most purposes, and there are some higher-output sports coils which will merely cause excessive points burning and possibly damage the electronic rev counter if fitted. A full-race engine – with a 649 cam and a 13:1 compression ratio, that sort of thing – may benefit from the use of a heavy duty coil such as, for example, one intended for six-cylinder cars like the Healey 3000. Out-and-out sports/racing equipment like the legendary 'red-topped' coil is only remotely necessary on a full-race Cooper S and even then it's a debatable point.

What is essential is that the HT lead should be connected to the coil through a screw-in cap, not just a push fit into the top. I have known too many instances of the latter type causing an intermittent misfire because of a faulty contact.

While purpose-built competition machinery increasingly uses various forms of electronic ignition system, there is no evidence that anything of the sort is really necessary on a Mini. There is a variety of add-on systems on the market from which you can choose if so inclined. When they are good, they are no doubt very good; but when they are bad, they are an added source of unreliability and elusive faults which the non-electrician may find it hard to trace. Given that the possible benefits are not overwhelming, my advice would be to concentrate on keeping the standard system in tip-top condition and spend your money first on other things.

High-tension leads

The HT leads from the coil to the distributor and from the distributor to the plugs can cause a variety of problems. People are not always aware of the propensity of the high-tension current to escape, given half a chance, and not find its way to the sparking plug. Look under the bonnet of some cars in the dark with the engine running and you will see something a bit like the Northern Lights as the sparks wander about on the surface of the leads!

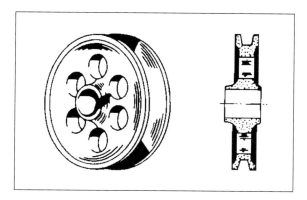

The large-diameter pulley used to reduce dynamo revs is very heavy but can be lightened by drilling and removing 20 to 25 thou from the sides, then given a final polish.

An annoying and not uncommon fault is an incurably irregular tick-over which, with the Mini transverse engine layout, often causes idler-gear knock. One cause lies with the fact that nearly all modern cars are equipped with HT leads intended to suppress radio and television interference and made of a textile fibre material impregnated with carbon. Unfortunately, the resistance to electric current offered by this material is very variable. If you check, you will quite often find as much as 50% difference in resistance between the leads on one engine, which causes a considerable variation in the strength of spark between the cylinders. The remedy is simple: replace all the leads with old-fashioned but nonetheless more reliable copper-core cable. Any variation in conductivity between copper leads can only be measured with the most sophisticated and delicate equipment.

Not only is the copper core more consistent (and less prone to damage and deterioration), it is also a better conductor as well, thus giving a stronger spark at the plug, particularly important on a high-compression, full-race engine. The only snag is that the dictates both of the law and of a responsible social attitude make radio and TV suppression necessary, so individual suppressors must be fitted to each lead. I have never known these to give any trouble when in good condition, but it's not a bad idea to replace them every couple of years.

Plug caps should be of the snug-fitting rubber variety, such as those coveted by the motorcycle brigade, and they should screw into the copper core of the leads. In addition to being waterproof, these caps, being a tight fit, make better contact with the plugs than some of the hard plastic ones. But they do perish with age, and should be replaced every three years or so.

Generator

Minis began with dynamos and then moved on, like most production cars, into the era of alternators. Needless to say, rallying enthusiasts invariable favour alternators, since they produce more current to satisfy the demand of all those extra lights. For road use, too, the rapid recharging rate after cold starting and the ease with which the system will cope with a few extra electrical accessories make the alternator preferable for most drivers, particularly in the winter.

But you don't get something for nothing. Not only are alternators more expensive in the first place, they also absorb up to 30% more engine power. As anyone who has studied the laws of physics will know, the extra electrical energy has to come from somewhere, and in this case it is converted by the alternator from mechanical energy which comes from the output of the engine and hence is not available to drive the wheels. If you can reduce the output of the generator, there will be more power to propel the car.

But this consideration is really only worthwhile on the most highly developed racing units and even then gains are very small. Before rushing out to alter the generator on your racer, make sure that the regulations allow such modifications. Mini 7 regs certainly didn't. Regulations permitting, you can even remove the generator altogether for short sprint or hillclimb events. (Don't forget you still need a belt to drive the water pump!) On longer events, reduction in battery output towards the end of the day can have an adverse affect on ignition efficiency and more than nullify any small gains from dispensing with the generator.

Engine rev limits have gone up way beyond what was normal when the standard dynamo first appeared, and there is a tendency for dynamos to burn themselves out at sustained high speeds. (Another advantage of alternators is their tolerance of much higher rotational speeds.) Fitting a larger dynamo pulley (part number C-AEA 535) reduces dynamo speed, and will necessitate the use of a longer fan belt, part number C-AEA 756. This reduces the risk of dynamo burning and gives a minute bonus in power available at the wheels, but with a fall in the charging rate at lower speeds, of course, so it is a racing-only modification. The replacement

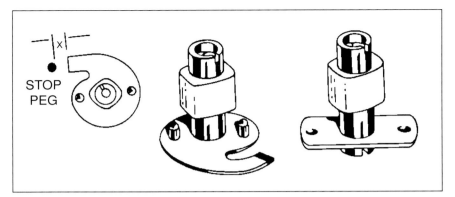

pulleys are very heavy and can be lightened with benefits to both the load on the dynamo bearings and the vehicle's overall weight.

Distributor

One of the most confusing aspects of engine modification is the problem of distributors. They all look alike but they are oh so different in detail, with different balance springs and advance plates giving differing advance characteristics. For our purposes, Mini distributors can be divided into four types. Within the types there are small differences only, but between the main types there is strictly limited interchangeability.

Commercial type (van and pick-up): These were designed for use with the cheapest grades of petrol, so they have only limited inbuilt advance. Consequently, provided one is prepared to use a higher grade of petrol (and inevitably anyway with the gradual disappearance of the lower grades), worthwhile improvements can be made simply by changing to the unit fitted to the equivalent car. Better fuel consumption often offsets any increase in cost. So, for example, it pays to change a Mini van distributor for a Mini 850 saloon type.

Car type (excluding 997 Cooper and Cooper S): With minor changes depending on the exact vehicle in question, this type is fitted to most A-series engines. Unless modifications to the engine include a change of camshaft, there is little point in changing the distributor. If, however, a more vigorous camshaft is to be fitted, then one of the following units should be used, assuming that the camshaft in question is of BMC/BLMC origin. With a cam from an independent specialist, consult the supplier: it may still be that one of the following is suitable.

997 Cooper and competition type **C-27H 7766**: Basically, both of these were designed for use with the 2A948 (now 88G229) camshaft which was fitted as standard to the 997cc Cooper. But the competition distributor is also suitable for use with the 731 cam or even the early full-race 544 cam.

Cooper S type: I can say without fear of contradiction that this unit represents the universally suitable distributor, provided that premium fuel is used. It is usable on anything from the standard 850 to a full-race Cooper S, and if ever I had to buy a new unit or modify an existing one then this is the distributor I would use.

The distributors are all interchangeable in the sense that they can be bolted on to any engine without further modifications to make them fit, though the Cooper S and competition units have no vacuum advance and retard mechanism. In fact, this is a worthwhile modification even on a standard engine: disconnect the vacuum pipe to prevent the possibility of over-advance and resultant engine damage. Remember to block the take-off hole in the manifold or carburettor choke tube. Another useful mod to any distributor is to fit a Cooper S contact-breaker kit. The points are better material and the spring is stronger which is useful if high revs are envisaged.

Even on exchange, distributors are quite expensive and as an outright purchase they cost a bomb. However, do not despair: in nearly all cases there is, with a little effort, a cheap way out. I will deal with the exception later. It is possible, at very low cost, to modify even the commercial vehicle distributor to any specification up to Cooper S standard.

First, open up your own unit and inspect the plate attached to the bottom of the cam rotor, the plate to which the springs and balance weights are attached. On the upper surface of this plate, by the beak, you will see stamped the maximum inbuilt mechanical advance of the distributor in degrees. Let us say that in your case this is 12 degrees.

If you partially dismantle the distributor you will find that after the top plate, to which the contact breaker is attached, has been removed another beaked plate will be exposed, this being an integral part of the distributor cam. Measure very carefully the distance between the leading edge of the beak and the stop peg; let's call it Xmm. Since Xmm is the distance moved by the beaked plate in advancing the ignition 12 degrees, Xmm divided by 12 will be the amount of movement needed to advance the ignition by one degree. In standard form, once your distributor has advanced 12 degrees, the beak comes up against the stop peg thus preventing further mechanical advance.

If, however, you were to grind X/12mm off the end of the beak, the amount of movement would increase by this amount and the advance would increase to 13 degrees. So it now becomes a simple matter to grind the appropriate amount from the beak to increase the amount of inbuilt advance to whatever you require. Find out what advance figure is stamped on the distributor you want to replicate, subtract the figure stamped on your unit, multiply the difference by your mm-per-degree factor (X/12 in our example) and you have the amount to be ground off the beak to achieve the extra advance needed.

The difference will rarely be more than 3 to 5 degrees. If you ask for the advance specification of a distributor, remember that it is the amount of inbuilt mechanical advance you want (usually between 10 and 15 degrees) not the overall advance where a vacuum mechanism is fitted nor the advance including static setting required by the engine for which it was designed. On a racing engine the latter figure could be as high as 35 degrees.

The mechanical advance is achieved by the centrifugal action of the balance weights pulling against the springs, so the correct spring tension is important too. Finish the job off by fitting a new set of balance-weight springs of the type fitted to the distributor the specification of which you were aiming at. Disconnect and preferably completely remove the vacuum mechanism, bellows and all, having first joined the upper and lower halves of the top plate together using solder and/or self-tapping screws. While it is not strictly necessary to take this mechanism off, it makes things look much neater, particularly if the resultant hole in the side of the distributor is neatly and carefully filled with epoxy resin filler.

When finished, you have built yourself the equivalent of a Cooper S distributor, or any other special type that you wanted, for a very small outlay. You could have started with any of the standard distributors, van, saloon, or what-have-you, with just one exception. One type of distributor (part number 2A 995) which was fitted to the earliest Minis in 1959 and early 1960 had different internal parts to those just described and cannot be modified, it can only be replaced complete. It can be recognized by the absence of a beak on the plate attached to the distributor cam: in this case the plate is much smaller and more oval.

19

Interchangeability

The extraordinarily long popularity which the Mini has enjoyed among enthusiasts, and the way in which it has continued to be seen in most forms of club motor sport long after the pundits had written it off as no longer competitive, result from a number of different factors. There is availability, sheer weight of numbers. Minis and bits for Minis can be found everywhere, and their following has ensured that they have received plenty of attention from the manufacturers of tuning equipment and aftermarket accessories as well.

Relative simplicity and low cost are important, too. With a few exceptions, most of the work likely to be needed on a Mini is within the scope of a reasonably competent do-it-yourselfer. Mini spares may not be cheaper than those for roughly comparable bread-and-butter cars, but they are certainly not as dear as those for some of the slightly more exotic sporting marques. And they are very adaptable: competitors are often able to use suitably modified standard components in applications where the adherents of other models are compelled to employ specially made bits at high cost. Racing Minis, for example, have mostly used one or other of the standard cylinder head castings, unlike downdraught Anglias and Fraser Imps.

The other major factor is interchangeability. Being able to swap bits from one Mini variant to another makes it possible to achieve the right combination for your own particular needs. The fact that some parts from the competition-orientated Cooper S can be employed on the lesser Minis has enabled them to become reliable

competition machines without the cost and complexity of one-off engineering. Some aspects of this adaptability have been covered already, but it could be useful to bring together some more observations on the subject.

Let's begin with the bodyshell. Basically, all Mini bodies are identical in all significant dimensions and shapes. There have been detail variations such as the larger rear window after September 1967, but virtually nothing which affects interchangeability. The mounting points for all the mechanical appendages are identical except that some models have the hole in the floor for the gearchange in a different place. That can soon be changed using a pair of tin-snips and an aluminium blanking plate. The earliest Minis, from 1959 to around May 1960, were about 40lb lighter because of thin-gauge steel used in the floor and seat, together with the absence of one or two minor structural plates which usually pass without being noticed by the inexperienced eye. The rear shock-absorber mountings on 1959 Minis were weak and had a nasty habit of giving way, letting the dampers up into the boot. No safety-belt mountings were included till about 1962. After 1965 the front valance was cut away at each side to allow cold air to get the brakes, the manufacturers following the lead of many club racers.

The vans, pick-ups and estates have a wheelbase 4in longer than the saloons, but it is only the sheet metal in the middle that is stretched: the mounting points at each end are all the same. Even the booted Elf and Hornet bodies are the same as the Mini in almost all their major dimensions, and accept the same mechanical components and subframes. There are no differences between the bodyshells of Hydrolastic and solid rubber-suspended Minis. If you write off a solid-rubber Mini, you rebuild it using the same shell as the chap with Hydrolastics.

By this time, some readers will be saying, 'The man's mad – what about the ones with the Clubman nose?' Well, the answer to that is that in actual fact the differences are much less than they might at first seem. Although there are no external door hinges, the shells are identical for all practical purposes from the front bulkhead seams backwards. A Mini of the ordinary shape can be converted to Clubman shape simply by fitting a new front end, something which the manufacturers of glassfibre body panels quickly realized. All the major mechanical parts including the subframes can be regarded as identical.

If you are using new subframes, then you use the same pattern, front and rear, whether the suspension is solid or Hydrolastic. The earlier subframes for solid-suspension cars were different in that there were no holes in them to take the hydraulic hoses, but later frames all have these holes so that they can be used as universal replacements. The frames are all the same for all models – van, saloon, Cooper S or whatever. With the suspension components themselves, though, things become a little more complicated.

Rear suspension

All major dimensions are the same and consequently most components are interchangeable, but later equipment is slightly different and in some cases superior. The massive iron swinging arms which carry the rear wheels are identical throughout the entire Mini range except for the fact that before about 1962 they were pivoted on plain bushes instead of the needle-roller bearings adopted subsequently. Many early Minis will have been converted by now, and certainly anyone building a car for competition would be well advised to use the needle-roller type because wear rates are much lower than with the original set-up. The plain bushed type of arm is no longer available.

The suspension struts or 'trumpets' were originally made of steel but were soon replaced by a cast alloy type which is not necessarily superior. These struts are completely interchangeable on solid rubber suspensions, though those fitted to vans and estates are 0.200in longer to give an increased ride height and need shortening, as detailed in the section on suspension lowering (Chapter 7), if used on a saloon. Hydrolastic Minis have rods instead of 'trumpets': they fit and operate in exactly the same way but are not interchangeable with the solid-suspension type.

The rubber suspension cones on all solid Minis and variants are theoretically identical, though very early (1959-60) cars had a different rubber mix: the part number remained unchanged. On Hydrolastic Minis, the rubber cones are replaced by the rubber and fluid Hydrolastic unit. These are interchangeable in terms of dimensions and fitting, but there have been several different ratings, as explained in Chapter 7. Swapping from solid to Hydrolastic or vice versa is possible, given drilled subframes, provided you use rods or 'trumpets' as appropriate and fit the correct shock absorbers or the necessary hydraulic paraphernalia for the Hydrolastic system.

Front suspension

Unfortunately there are more limits to interchangeability at the front end of the Mini than at the back, but there is still a fair bit of scope for imagination. All rubber cones on the solid Minis are interchangeable, as are the struts or 'trumpets', just as at the rear, and the remarks made for the Hydrolastic rear suspension apply at the front too. The top suspension arms are all similar and interchangeable, except that the Hydrolastic type have no shock-absorber mountings on them. This is easy to rectify, the arms themselves being otherwise the same.

The bottom arms are, again, all very similar right across the range. The only variation is that the later pattern arm has a larger eye at the inner end to accept the later type of rubber bush which has a steel insert intended to lengthen its life and provide better location. You simply use the appropriate type of bush for the arms you are fitting. It is these lower arms which are lengthened to obtain negative camber at the front wheels, and it is worth emphasizing again that any such modification must be carried out with the greatest care to eliminate any possibility of breakage.

The tie bars which link the outer ends of the lower arms to the front of the subframe are identical on all Minis. By varying the thickness of the inner rubber bush, and/or the washers between the car and subframe, one can alter the front wheel castor angle.

The steering arms, which link the front hubs to the rack, are all interchangeable but there is more than one type. The Cooper S (after the first few produced) has arms of increased diameter for greater strength, and fitting those is obviously a good idea when using a Mini in competition. With the Mk2 Mini a modified steering rack was introduced and this necessitated a change in the steering arms, so arms and rack must match to produce the correct geometry.

Many competitors have stuck to their preference for the solid rubber type of suspension when racing or rallying the Mini. It is easier to set up and about 100lb lighter – and there is less to break, too. On the other hand, some of the quickest racing Minis ever produced, like the Alec Poole Hornet, the Janspeed SCA and the Harry Ratcliffe Vita-D 1300 used Hydrolastic suspension. Special competition units were produced by the manufacturer.

Brakes

In this field there is a very, very wide choice if you take into account all the possible variations in wheel cylinders, linings and so on. But for the sake of simplicity, we can make several broad divisions based on model and brake size.

Narrow drum brakes. These were fitted to all Mini saloons, vans and estates up to 1964, and were of the single-leading-shoe variety. On a very early Mini, it pays to use the improved, 1964-pattern wheel cylinders used on the last of the single-leading-shoe brakes: they can be fitted as straightforward replacements.

Wider drum brakes. These were fitted on all non-Cooper Minis, including vans and estates, after September 1964, and on all Elf and Hornet models (except possibly a few of the very first produced). The distinguishing feature is that the front brakes had a twin-leading-shoe layout, with two cylinders each side instead of the earlier one. It is perfectly possible to fit this pattern to an earlier car, but the backplates are not the same so you have to obtain the complete backplate with cylinders and the extra pipe. In fact the drums on all drum-braked Minis are identical: it was only the shoes and linings which were widened to increase the friction area. But, if carrying out a conversion, it will be necessary to fit new drums as well, because the narrower shoes will have worn the contact areas in the drums. It is possible to clean the old drums up, if they are not too deeply worn, by skimming up to a maximum of 0.030in off the inner surface, but I proved that this is unsafe, certainly for racing. Minifin light-alloy drums are an alternative worth considering if new drums are to be fitted.

Mini-Cooper. Rear drum brakes as on other Minis are fitted, together with front disc brakes. The first pattern, on 997cc Coopers, were worse than useless: those fitted to 998cc Coopers are much better, having larger calipers which can easily be fitted to a 997cc car. Cooper discs can be fitted to any other non-S Mini, by utilizing the complete hub assemblies, without needing other alterations apart from suitable brake fluid and possibly a master cylinder with a larger fluid reservoir. As explained earlier in the book, however, it is a conversion of no practical use, in my opinion, and certainly inadequate for competition.

Cooper S. Again a disc front and drum rear layout, but much better, with larger discs. The rear drums contain the wider linings and have integral wheel spacers: while these will fit an ordinary Mini, they are very heavy and I would prefer to use ordinary drums with alloy spacers or the Minifin type, giving a significant saving in weight. Cooper S disc front brakes cannot be fitted to any other Mini without also fitting Cooper S hubs, uprights, drive-shafts and master cylinder. Even the flexible hoses are different, the correct type, identified by a double green band, being stronger and less likely to swell under pressure.

Front hubs

There have been a few changes to the front hub and wheel bearing assembly. The number of splines on early Mini drive-shafts differed from later models and consequently the hubs were different too. Disc brakes demand different hubs from drum brakes. The Cooper S has larger, stronger hub bearings from other models, again needing a different hub. As already indicated in relation to brakes, interchangeability in this area is in general a matter of swapping complete assemblies rather than individual components.

Drive-shafts

Apart from the early change in the number of splines which has already been mentioned, the principal distinction in Mini drive-shafts is between the original rubber-cross inboard universal joint, which remained standard on all ordinary Minis for many years, and the Hardy-Spicer joint used on the Cooper S and also on automatic-transmission cars. Increasing the power output obviously puts greater strain on the drive-shaft joints, and while the rubber-cross pattern is adequate for the smaller-capacity units, and for 850 racers, the Hardy-Spicer type is necessary for the largest engines and for serious competition work with all but an 850. Changing to the Hardy-Spicer type, however, necessitates changing the drive flanges on the differential which in turn means replacing most of the internal components of the diff, so it is less simple and considerably more costly than might at first appear. A useful half-way house is the Quinton-Hazel kit which replaces the rubber-cross joint with a stronger roller-bearing spider joint very much like the propeller-shaft joints on a conventional rear-wheel-drive car, without the need to change shafts or flanges.

Fitting a limited-slip differential will almost certainly mean using Hardy-Spicer drive-shaft joints. There was an early limited-slip assembly designed to accept the rubber-cross joints, but you could have difficulty finding one. In any application where joints of the rubber-cross pattern are to be subjected to heavier-than-

normal wear and tear, frequent checks on their condition are advisable as they may well prove to have a limited life.

While the drive flanges on the differential are different for the two types of drive-shaft joint, the splines on the shafts themselves are not (except in the case of the early cars already mentioned). So if, for example, you want to fit a Cooper S front-end to a car with rubber universal joints, the Hardy-Spicer flanges can easily be slid off the Cooper S drive-shafts and the rubber-cross type flanges fitted in their place.

Using Cooper S parts
As already indicated, it is relatively easy to fit Cooper S front brakes to other Minis providing you use the appropriate hubs, uprights, drive-shafts and so on. A by-product of this conversion is wider front track and you will need to widen the

A full field of Mini racers streams down the hill from Druids at Brands Hatch, Richard Longman in the lead.

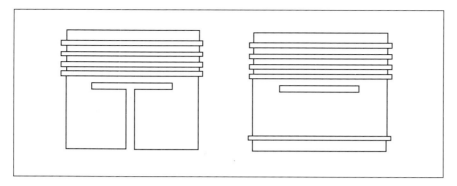

Split-skirt (left) and solid-skirt pistons. The additional skirt ring shown on the right-hand example is simply a source of additional friction.

rear track to match. The cheapest and lightest way of doing this is to fit wheel spacers at least ¾in thick to the standard rear drums. You can use Cooper S rear drums but they are heavy, expensive if purchased separately, and offer no real advantage that I can see. In either case, it is necessary to fit longer wheel studs to the rear hubs.

Fitting the stronger S-type steering arms is a good idea, and essential for competition. But remember that the change in steering-arm geometry around the autumn of 1967 affected the S too, so do not use the later S steering arms on an earlier car.

The Cooper S hub assemblies position the steering arms further away from the centre-line of the car than the ordinary pattern, so the tracking will have to be re-adjusted. The track-rod ends may need to be screwed so far of the rack tie-rods that not enough thread remains to hold them safely together – there must be at least ⅜in of thread still engaged. Modifying the suspension to add negative camber at the front wheels makes this problem still more acute. There are two possible solutions. One is to lengthen the track-rod ends: obtain two new ones – the originals will probably be rusty – and two new locking nuts to suit. Screw a locking nut onto a suitable bolt and screw the track-rod end on after it until the two are tight together. Then get them nickel-bronze welded together: the result is a track-rod end longer by the thickness of the nut, and it can be fitted and locked in the usual manner. This method has been proven quite safe and reliable by many racing enthusiasts. However, if serious rallying, autocross or rallycross is envisaged, I would recommend the alternative but more expensive method, which is to remove the tie rods from the rack and get some special, longer ones made to take their place. A Mini tuning specialist might be able to help.

Engine components

Some examples of the interchangeability of engine components have already come up in the course of describing specific tuning methods for the different sizes of Mini power unit. The total number of possible permutations is so great that I cannot cover them all, and many would have little practical application. But the following points are important.

As we have already seen, the 850 Mini has connecting rods fitted with pinch-bolt little ends. It is quite straightforward to fit 998 or 1100-pattern fully floating rods, but either the pistons must be changed or the 850 pistons need to have circlip grooves machined in them and the internal distance between the gudgeon-pin bosses increased. The appropriate 1100 gudgeon pins (or 948cc Triumph Herald pins) are of course required as well.

Given that 850 piston modification, all Mini connecting rods other than Cooper S and non-S 1275 ones are identical in their major dimensions and interchangeable. Cooper S rods should only be used on S engines, and there are two different types. The 1275 and 1071 ones are similar, but those for the 970 are longer.

It's worth mentioning at this stage that the 1275 Cooper S block is taller than the 1071 and 970, which are identical. Later 1275 Cooper S engines have strengthened main-bearing housings and cross-drilled crankshafts.

The only specifically Cooper S engine parts that are easily fitted to other A-series engines are valve-gear components and the cylinder head, though whether the latter is worthwhile is a matter for debate. The Sprite Mk3 1,098cc block, with its 2in main-bearing journals, does make it possible to construct hybrid engines utilizing major Cooper S components, but there is little to be gained on anything with a capacity other than between 1,100 and 1,200cc.

It is possible to fit the crankshaft from a 997, 998 or 1,098cc engine to an 850 Mini block, but the main-bearing housing needs thinning down to make room. In my opinion this is a waste of time, though: it is cheaper, easier and better to change the whole engine for a 998 or 1,098cc unit. 998 and 1,098cc cranks (but not the 2in main type) can be swapped, which may be a useful exercise, but the pistons will need changing too, the 998 ones being taller.

On the relationship between block height, stroke, capacity and piston type, note the following:

A: All A-series blocks other than Cooper S are the same height, and similar in all other outside dimensions and most internal ones.

B: The 850 has its own bore and stroke, but only the stroke differs between 998 and 1,098cc engines. Since the block height and connecting rod lengths are the same, the shorter the stroke, the taller the piston, and vice versa.

C: Compression ratios are varied on standard production versions by changing the degree of dishing in the top of the piston.

To illustrate the practical implications of all this, let us put together some hypothetical engine assemblies.

1: 850 block and crank, 1100 rods and pistons. Rods, block and crank pose no problem; most blocks can be bored to take 1100 pistons. So far, so good, but – the pistons were intended for an engine with a stroke of some 83mm, while the 850 stroke is 68mm odd. So there is a difference in stroke of about 15mm and, as already explained, with no change in block height or rod length, this must be accommodated by a difference in piston height. The 1100 pistons must be shorter by about 7.5mm (half the stroke difference) than those of the 850, measured from the gudgeon pin centre to the crown. Consequently at top dead centre they would not reach the top of the bore – only about 3 or 4mm at most can be shaved off the top face of the block – so this engine cannot be built unless non-standard pistons can be obtained.

2: Sprite Mk3 block (bore dimension as per 998 and 1100 engines), 1071 S crankshaft, 1100 rods, 998 dished pistons. As the Mk3 engine has 2in-diameter main bearings and bore centres are not too dissimilar, the S crank and this block will mate up all right. The 1071 S stroke is the same as an 850, approximately 68mm. The 998 stroke

is 76mm so the difference in piston height is only 4mm, and that amount can be machined from the top of some (though not all) blocks to enable the pistons to reach the tops of the bores. So this combination could work.

One motive which leads people to this kind of mixing and matching of bits and pieces from different versions of the A-series engine is increasing the cubic capacity in search of more power. The attraction of gaining increased power this way is that, with suitable camshaft and carburation changes, it is mid-range torque and drivability that benefit, not just top-end bhp. Beyond the limits set by the dimensions of standard components, further increases can only be obtained by overboring the block. The best guide on how much the bore dimension can safely be increased is to find out just how far the specialist tuners are willing to go, so that you can profit by the experience of their past mistakes. Remember, however, that a percentage of engines bored to the supposed maximum are rendered useless because of porosity in the cylinder wall resulting from casting irregularities in production. In practical terms, too, the availability of suitable pistons is often the determining factor.

On the subject of pistons, it is sometimes assumed that the solid-skirt type automatically result in more power, but there is no reason why this should be the case. Unless they are very carefully machined, with ovalized skirts, the only real gains are in reliability at high revs, when the danger of piston breakage is reduced. Neither is it necessarily true that split skirts cause power losses.

But extra piston rings do consume more power. Pistons fitted with skirt rings, as some of the commoner solid-skirt pistons are, have a definite disadvantage in the form of increased friction. If an engine uses oil, the remedy is to have it rebored and use properly fitting pistons and rings – extra rings are not the way to do it. New engines do not normally burn oil, after running in, nor do they have pistons with skirt rings. By reboring and renewing the pistons you should in effect return to new specification. If the engine still burns oil, something is wrong with the boring or the assembly, in which case, march it back to the supplier. Check first, however, that the oil is not being lost elsewhere, through leakage, for example, or worn valve guides.

ALSO FROM MRP . . .

THE SPORTING MINIS: A COLLECTOR'S GUIDE. John Brigden. The ideal companion to this book. Covers the Mini-Cooper, Mini-Cooper S and 1275GT, with full production and competition history, information on choice and restoration, and detailed specifications, performance figures and production data. 120 pages, 180 x 235mm, 130 illus. Casebound.
0 947981 40 3   £12.95

THEORY AND PRACTICE OF CYLINDER HEAD MODIFICATION. David Vizard. Intended both as a textbook for the engineering student and as a guide for the practical enthusiast. Imparts much wisdom gathered during the author's many years in the tuning business. Includes actual size drawings of the heads of many popular engines with recommended modifications. 176 pages, 214 x 140mm, approx. 100 illus. Softbound.
085113066 6   £7.95

PRACTICAL GAS FLOW: TECHNIQUES FOR LOW-BUDGET PERFORMANCE TUNING. John Dalton. Describes how the do-it-yourself tuner can check the gas flow in an engine, devise improvements and test and compare their effect. Explains an ingenious modelling technique for experimenting with cylinder-head modification. 112 pages, 246 x 186mm, 75 illus. Casebound.
0 947981 33 0   £9.95

AUTOMOTIVE GLASSFIBRE. Dennis Foy. A step-by-step handbook for the DIY person who wants to repair, restore, modify or improve the body of a road car, competition car, street machine or special. Covers workshop set-up, tools, materials, techniques, safety and other essentials. 192 pages, 215 x 135mm, 130 illus. Casebound.
0 947981 19 5   £9.95

HANDLING AND ROADHOLDING: CAR SUSPENSION AT WORK. Jeffrey Daniels. Explains clearly and authoritatively the science of chassis performance and the related aspects of car handling, roadholding, ride and response. An important book for all enthusiastic drivers and students of car technology, with many specially executed drawings. 160 pages, 246 x 186mm, approx. 120 illus. Casebound.
0 947981 22 5   £14.95

These are just a few examples from the extensive MRP list of tuning and modification books, restoration guides, driving manuals and in-depth model histories, a prime source of interest and information for all motoring enthusiasts. For full details, please write for a free catalogue to:

MOTOR RACING PUBLICATIONS LTD, UNIT 6, THE PILTON ESTATE, 46 PITLAKE, CROYDON, SURREY, CR0 3RA Telephone 081-681 3363/2255